MASTERING ARTIFICIAL INTELLIGENCE

From a Noob to an AI Expert

Yatendra Kumar Singh "Manuh"

CONTENTS

INTRODUCTION

The world of Artificial Intelligence (AI) is vast and constantly evolving, touching every aspect of our lives. From healthcare and finance to entertainment and agriculture, AI is reshaping industries, enhancing productivity, and enabling innovative solutions to complex problems. This book aims to provide a comprehensive understanding of AI, its applications, ethical considerations, and future trends. Whether you are a seasoned professional, a student, or simply someone curious about AI, this book will guide you through the fascinating journey of artificial intelligence.

Understanding AI

At its core, AI is the science of creating machines that can perform tasks that typically require human intelligence. These tasks include learning, reasoning, problem-solving, perception, and natural language understanding. AI systems leverage vast amounts of data, advanced algorithms, and powerful computing resources to analyze information, make decisions, and learn from experiences. The rapid advancements in AI have led to its widespread adoption across various sectors, driving innovation and transforming how we live and work.

The Importance of AI

AI holds immense potential for addressing some of the most pressing challenges of our time. In healthcare, AI-powered diagnostics and personalized treatments are improving patient outcomes and saving lives. In finance, AI-driven algorithms are enhancing risk management, automating trading, and providing personalized financial services. In agriculture, AI is promoting sustainable farming practices, optimizing resource use, and increasing crop yields. The impact of AI extends to many other fields, including transportation, education, customer service, and environmental sustainability.

Ethical Considerations

As AI continues to advance, it is crucial to address the ethical considerations associated with its development and deployment. Ensuring that AI systems are fair, transparent, accountable, and respect privacy is essential for building trust and promoting positive societal impact. This book explores the ethical principles guiding AI research and development and provides strategies for addressing ethical challenges in various applications.

The Future of AI

The future of AI is filled with exciting possibilities and challenges. Emerging trends such as explainable AI, AI-driven automation, edge AI, and AI for climate change are shaping the next generation of AI technologies. Potential breakthroughs in artificial general intelligence (AGI), neuromorphic computing, federated learning, and AI-enhanced creativity are pushing the boundaries of what AI can achieve. As we look to the future, it is essential to harness the power of AI responsibly and ethically to ensure that its benefits are realized for all.

Structure of the Book

This book is organized into comprehensive chapters, each focusing on a specific aspect of AI. From foundational concepts and key techniques to practical applications and future trends, each chapter provides in-depth insights and practical knowledge. Real-world examples, case studies, and best practices are included to illustrate the transformative potential of AI in various domains.

Who Should Read This Book

This book is designed for a diverse audience, including:

- **Professionals and Practitioners:** Individuals working in AI, data science, and related fields who seek to deepen their understanding and stay updated on the latest trends and advancements.

- **Students and Researchers:** Students, academics, and researchers looking for a comprehensive resource on AI concepts, applications, and ethical considerations.

- **Business Leaders and Decision Makers:** Executives and managers who want to leverage AI to drive innovation, improve efficiency, and gain a competitive edge.

- **Enthusiasts and Curious Minds:** Anyone interested in exploring the fascinating world of AI and its impact on various aspects of our lives.

Conclusion

The journey of AI is ongoing, and its impact on society continues to grow. By understanding the principles, applications, and ethical considerations of AI, we can harness its potential to address global challenges, drive innovation, and create a better future for all. This book is your guide to navigating the dynamic and transformative world of artificial intelligence. Let's embark on this journey together and explore the limitless possibilities of

AI.

◆ ◆ ◆

CHAPTER 1: WHAT IS ARTIFICIAL INTELLIGENCE?

Overview

Artificial Intelligence (AI) is one of the most transformative technologies of our time, reshaping industries and redefining the way we live and work. This chapter provides an introduction to AI, its definition, scope, and significance. We will explore the historical development of AI, its core components, and its diverse applications across various sectors.

Definition and Scope

Definition: Artificial Intelligence refers to the simulation of human intelligence processes by machines, especially computer systems. These processes include learning (the acquisition of information and rules for using the information), reasoning (using rules to reach approximate or definite conclusions), and self-correction.

Scope: AI encompasses a wide range of technologies and approaches, including machine learning, natural language processing, computer vision, robotics, and more. The scope of AI extends from simple automation to complex problem-solving and decision-making processes. AI can be categorized into three main types:

1. **Narrow AI (Weak AI):** AI systems designed and trained for a specific task, such as image recognition or language translation.

2. **General AI (Strong AI):** Hypothetical AI that possesses the ability to perform any intellectual task that a human can do.

3. **Superintelligent AI:** An advanced form of AI that surpasses human intelligence in all aspects, including creativity, general wisdom, and problem-solving.

History of AI

Early Beginnings: The concept of intelligent machines dates back to ancient mythology, but the formal study of AI began in the mid-20th century. Key milestones in the history of AI include:

- **1943:** Warren McCulloch and Walter Pitts published a seminal paper on artificial neurons, laying the groundwork for neural networks.
- **1950:** Alan Turing introduced the Turing Test, a criterion for determining whether a machine can exhibit human-like intelligence.
- **1956:** The term "Artificial Intelligence" was coined at the Dartmouth Conference, which is considered the birth of AI as an academic discipline.

The Evolution of AI: AI has undergone several periods of significant progress and setbacks, often referred to as "AI winters" and "AI springs." Notable developments include:

- **1960s-1970s:** Early AI research focused on symbolic AI and rule-based systems.
- **1980s:** The rise of expert systems, which used knowledge-based approaches to solve complex problems in specific domains.
- **1990s:** The emergence of machine learning, which emphasized data-driven approaches and statistical methods.
- **2000s-Present:** Advances in deep learning, natural language processing, and computational power have

led to breakthroughs in various AI applications.

Importance and Applications of AI

Importance of AI: AI is driving innovation and efficiency across multiple industries, offering numerous benefits such as:

- **Automation:** AI can automate repetitive and mundane tasks, freeing up human workers to focus on more complex and creative endeavors.
- **Enhanced Decision-Making:** AI systems can analyze vast amounts of data to provide insights and recommendations, improving decision-making processes.
- **Personalization:** AI enables personalized experiences in fields like marketing, healthcare, and education, tailoring services to individual needs.
- **Innovation:** AI is a catalyst for innovation, enabling the development of new products, services, and business models.

Applications of AI: AI is being applied in a wide range of sectors, including:

- **Healthcare:** AI-powered diagnostic tools, personalized treatment plans, and drug discovery.
- **Finance:** Fraud detection, algorithmic trading, and personalized financial advice.
- **Retail:** Customer service chatbots, inventory management, and personalized marketing.
- **Transportation:** Autonomous vehicles, traffic management systems, and logistics optimization.
- **Education:** Intelligent tutoring systems, personalized learning, and administrative automation.
- **Entertainment:** Content recommendation engines, virtual reality, and game development.

Conclusion

Artificial Intelligence is a rapidly evolving field with the potential to revolutionize the way we live and work. From its early beginnings to its current advancements, AI has made significant strides in enhancing automation, decision-making, personalization, and innovation across various industries. In this chapter, we have explored the definition, scope, history, importance, and applications of AI. As we delve deeper into the subsequent chapters, we will uncover the intricacies of AI technologies, techniques, and their practical implementations.

In the next chapter, we will explore the differences between AI and human intelligence, examining the strengths and limitations of both, and discussing the ethical considerations surrounding AI development and use.

CHAPTER 2:
AI VS. HUMAN
INTELLIGENCE

Overview

As artificial intelligence (AI) continues to evolve, it is essential to understand how it compares to human intelligence. This chapter explores the differences between AI and human intelligence, examining their strengths and limitations. We will also discuss the ethical considerations surrounding AI development and use, which are crucial for ensuring responsible and beneficial advancements in this field.

Defining Human Intelligence

Human Intelligence: Human intelligence encompasses a broad range of cognitive abilities, including reasoning, problem-solving, learning, perception, creativity, and emotional understanding. It is a dynamic and adaptive system that allows individuals to navigate complex social environments, communicate effectively, and make informed decisions based on context and experience.

Key aspects of human intelligence include:

- **Cognitive Abilities:** The mental processes involved in acquiring knowledge and understanding through thought, experience, and the senses.
- **Emotional Intelligence:** The ability to recognize, understand, and manage one's own emotions and the

emotions of others.

- **Creativity:** The capacity to generate novel and valuable ideas, solutions, and artistic expressions.
- **Consciousness:** The state of being aware of and able to think about one's own existence, thoughts, and experiences.

Comparing AI and Human Intelligence

Strengths of AI:

1. **Processing Power:** AI can process vast amounts of data at incredible speeds, far surpassing human capabilities. This enables AI to perform complex calculations, analyze large datasets, and identify patterns that may not be apparent to humans.

2. **Consistency:** AI systems can perform tasks with high accuracy and consistency, without being influenced by fatigue, emotions, or biases that can affect human performance.

3. **Automation:** AI can automate repetitive and mundane tasks, freeing up human workers to focus on more creative and strategic activities.

4. **Scalability:** AI solutions can be scaled to handle increased workloads and expand across various applications and industries.

Limitations of AI:

1. **Lack of Common Sense:** AI systems often lack the common sense and contextual understanding that humans possess. This can lead to errors or inappropriate responses in situations that require nuanced judgment.

2. **Emotional Understanding:** AI lacks genuine emotional intelligence and cannot truly understand or empathize with human emotions. While AI can recognize emotional cues, it does not experience

emotions.

3. **Creativity:** AI can generate creative outputs based on patterns and data, but it does not possess intrinsic creativity or the ability to experience inspiration in the same way humans do.

4. **Ethical and Moral Reasoning:** AI operates based on predefined rules and algorithms, which can limit its ability to navigate complex ethical and moral dilemmas that require human judgment.

Strengths of Human Intelligence:

1. **Adaptability:** Humans can adapt to new and unforeseen situations, using their intuition, creativity, and experience to solve problems and make decisions.

2. **Emotional Intelligence:** Humans can understand and manage their own emotions and empathize with others, allowing for effective communication and interpersonal relationships.

3. **Common Sense:** Humans possess common sense, which enables them to navigate everyday situations and make contextually appropriate decisions.

4. **Moral and Ethical Reasoning:** Humans can consider ethical and moral implications when making decisions, taking into account social norms, cultural values, and personal principles.

Limitations of Human Intelligence:

1. **Cognitive Biases:** Human decision-making is often influenced by cognitive biases, which can lead to errors in judgment and reasoning.

2. **Limitations in Processing:** Humans have limited capacity to process large amounts of data quickly and accurately. This can hinder their ability to analyze complex information and identify patterns.

3. **Fatigue and Emotions:** Human performance can be

affected by fatigue, stress, and emotions, leading to inconsistencies and errors in task execution.

Ethical Considerations in AI

Bias and Fairness: AI systems can inherit biases present in the data they are trained on, leading to unfair and discriminatory outcomes. It is crucial to ensure that AI systems are designed and trained to minimize bias and promote fairness. This involves:

- **Diverse and Representative Data:** Ensuring that training data is diverse and representative of the population to avoid reinforcing existing biases.
- **Transparent Algorithms:** Developing transparent and explainable algorithms that allow for scrutiny and accountability.
- **Continuous Monitoring:** Regularly monitoring AI systems for biased outcomes and making necessary adjustments to mitigate bias.

Privacy and Security: AI systems often require large amounts of data, raising concerns about privacy and data security. Protecting individuals' privacy and ensuring data security are essential for maintaining trust in AI technologies. This involves:

- **Data Minimization:** Collecting and using only the data necessary for the intended purpose.
- **Encryption and Anonymization:** Implementing encryption and anonymization techniques to protect sensitive information.
- **Compliance with Regulations:** Adhering to privacy and data protection regulations, such as GDPR and CCPA.

Accountability and Responsibility: As AI systems become more autonomous, questions about accountability and responsibility arise. It is important to establish clear guidelines for accountability and ensure that humans remain responsible for the actions and decisions of AI systems. This involves:

- **Human Oversight:** Maintaining human oversight and control over AI systems, especially in critical and high-stakes applications.
- **Ethical Frameworks:** Developing and adhering to ethical frameworks that guide the responsible development and use of AI.
- **Transparency:** Being transparent about the capabilities and limitations of AI systems, as well as their decision-making processes.

Conclusion

Artificial intelligence and human intelligence have distinct strengths and limitations. While AI excels in processing power, consistency, and automation, it lacks the common sense, emotional understanding, and ethical reasoning that characterize human intelligence. Understanding these differences is crucial for leveraging the strengths of both AI and human intelligence to achieve complementary and beneficial outcomes.

In this chapter, we explored the key differences between AI and human intelligence, as well as the ethical considerations surrounding AI development and use. As we move forward, it is essential to continue developing AI technologies responsibly, ensuring that they align with human values and contribute to the betterment of society.

In the next chapter, we will delve into the different types of artificial intelligence, including narrow AI, general AI, and superintelligent AI. We will examine their characteristics, capabilities, and potential implications for the future.

CHAPTER 3: TYPES OF ARTIFICIAL INTELLIGENCE

Overview

Artificial Intelligence (AI) can be classified into various types based on its capabilities, complexity, and intended applications. Understanding these different types helps us appreciate the diversity within the field of AI and provides insight into the potential and limitations of each type. This chapter explores the three primary types of AI: Narrow AI, General AI, and Superintelligent AI. We will examine their characteristics, capabilities, current state, and potential implications for the future.

Narrow AI (Weak AI)

Definition: Narrow AI, also known as Weak AI, is designed and trained to perform specific tasks. It operates within a limited domain and cannot function beyond the tasks it has been programmed or trained to perform. Narrow AI excels in its specialized area but lacks general cognitive abilities.

Characteristics:

- **Specialized Functionality:** Narrow AI is tailored to perform particular tasks, such as image recognition, language translation, or recommendation systems.
- **No Self-Awareness:** Narrow AI lacks self-awareness, consciousness, and genuine understanding. It operates

based on predefined algorithms and patterns.

- **High Efficiency:** Narrow AI can perform its designated tasks with high efficiency and accuracy, often surpassing human capabilities in those specific areas.

Examples:

- **Image Recognition:** AI models like Convolutional Neural Networks (CNNs) are used for tasks such as facial recognition and object detection.

- **Natural Language Processing (NLP):** Language models like GPT-3 and chatbots like Microsoft's Copilot can understand and generate human language, but only within predefined contexts.

- **Recommendation Systems:** AI algorithms that recommend products, movies, or music based on user preferences and behavior.

Current State: Narrow AI is the most prevalent form of AI in use today. It powers many of the applications and services we interact with daily, such as virtual assistants (e.g., Siri, Alexa), autonomous vehicles, and fraud detection systems.

General AI (Strong AI)

Definition: General AI, also known as Strong AI or Artificial General Intelligence (AGI), refers to AI systems that possess the ability to understand, learn, and apply knowledge across a wide range of tasks and domains, similar to human cognitive abilities. General AI aims to achieve human-like intelligence and adaptability.

Characteristics:

- **Broad Cognitive Abilities:** General AI can perform any intellectual task that a human can do, including reasoning, problem-solving, and understanding complex concepts.

- **Self-Awareness:** General AI possesses self-awareness and consciousness, allowing it to understand and reflect on its own existence and actions.

- **Learning and Adaptation:** General AI can learn from experiences, adapt to new situations, and transfer knowledge across different domains.

Examples: As of now, General AI remains a theoretical concept, and no AI system has achieved the level of cognitive abilities required to be classified as General AI. Researchers and scientists continue to explore the possibilities and challenges of developing AGI.

Potential Implications:

- **Revolutionary Applications:** General AI has the potential to revolutionize industries by performing tasks that require human-like understanding and creativity.

- **Ethical and Philosophical Questions:** The development of General AI raises important ethical and philosophical questions about the nature of consciousness, the rights of AI entities, and the impact on human society.

- **Safety and Control:** Ensuring the safety and control of General AI is a significant concern, as its capabilities could pose risks if not managed responsibly.

Superintelligent AI

Definition: Superintelligent AI refers to an advanced form of AI that surpasses human intelligence in all aspects, including creativity, general wisdom, and problem-solving. Superintelligent AI would have the ability to outperform the best human minds in every field.

Characteristics:

- **Superior Cognitive Abilities:** Superintelligent AI possesses cognitive abilities far beyond those of humans, enabling it to solve complex problems and generate innovative solutions.

- **Self-Improvement:** Superintelligent AI can continuously improve itself, leading to rapid advancements in its capabilities.
- **Independent Goal-Setting:** Superintelligent AI can set its own goals and pursue them independently, potentially without human intervention.

Examples: As with General AI, Superintelligent AI remains a speculative concept and has not been realized. It is a subject of ongoing research and debate within the AI community.

Potential Implications:

- **Transformative Impact:** Superintelligent AI could transform society in unprecedented ways, addressing global challenges such as disease, poverty, and climate change.
- **Existential Risks:** The development of Superintelligent AI poses significant existential risks, including the potential loss of human control and unintended consequences.
- **Ethical Considerations:** The creation and governance of Superintelligent AI require careful ethical considerations to ensure that its development benefits humanity and avoids harm.

Conclusion

Understanding the different types of artificial intelligence —Narrow AI, General AI, and Superintelligent AI—provides valuable insights into the capabilities, limitations, and potential implications of each type. While Narrow AI is already prevalent in various applications, General AI and Superintelligent AI remain theoretical concepts that researchers continue to explore.

In this chapter, we have examined the characteristics, current state, and future implications of Narrow AI, General AI, and Superintelligent AI. As we progress through the subsequent chapters, we will delve deeper into specific AI techniques, technologies, and their practical applications.

In the next chapter, we will explore AI terminology and concepts, providing a foundational understanding of key terms and principles essential for comprehending the complexities of artificial intelligence.

CHAPTER 4: AI TERMINOLOGY AND CONCEPTS

Overview

To understand the complex and evolving field of Artificial Intelligence (AI), it is essential to familiarize yourself with the key terminology and concepts. This chapter serves as a foundational guide to the most important terms and principles in AI, providing a solid basis for further exploration of the subject.

Key Terms and Definitions

1. **Algorithm:**
    - A step-by-step procedure or set of rules designed to perform a specific task or solve a problem. Algorithms are the building blocks of AI systems.

2. **Machine Learning (ML):**
    - A subset of AI that involves the development of algorithms that allow machines to learn from and make predictions or decisions based on data. ML focuses on creating models that improve their performance over time without being explicitly programmed.

3. **Deep Learning:**
    - A subset of machine learning that uses neural

networks with multiple layers (hence "deep") to learn and make decisions. Deep learning is particularly effective in tasks such as image and speech recognition.

4. **Neural Network**:
   - A computational model inspired by the structure and function of the human brain. Neural networks consist of interconnected layers of nodes (neurons) that process and transmit information.

5. **Supervised Learning**:
   - A type of machine learning where the model is trained on labeled data. The model learns to map input data to the correct output based on the provided labels.

6. **Unsupervised Learning**:
   - A type of machine learning where the model is trained on unlabeled data. The model identifies patterns and relationships within the data without prior knowledge of the correct output.

7. **Reinforcement Learning**:
   - A type of machine learning where an agent learns to make decisions by interacting with its environment. The agent receives rewards or penalties based on its actions and aims to maximize cumulative rewards.

8. **Natural Language Processing (NLP)**:
   - A field of AI that focuses on the interaction between computers and human language. NLP involves tasks such as language understanding, language generation, and sentiment analysis.

9. **Computer Vision:**
    - A field of AI that enables machines to interpret and understand visual information from the world. Computer vision tasks include image recognition, object detection, and facial recognition.

10. **Artificial Neural Network (ANN):**
    - A neural network consisting of layers of artificial neurons. ANNs are used in various AI applications, including pattern recognition and classification.

11. **Convolutional Neural Network (CNN):**
    - A type of neural network designed for processing structured grid data, such as images. CNNs are widely used in image recognition and computer vision tasks.

12. **Recurrent Neural Network (RNN):**
    - A type of neural network designed for processing sequential data. RNNs are commonly used in tasks such as language modeling and time series prediction.

13. **Generative Adversarial Network (GAN):**
    - A type of neural network architecture consisting of two networks: a generator and a discriminator. GANs are used for generating realistic data, such as images and videos.

14. **Feature Extraction:**
    - The process of transforming raw data into a set of features that can be used for training a machine learning model. Feature extraction is a crucial step in data preprocessing.

15. **Hyperparameter:**
    - Parameters that define the structure and

behavior of a machine learning model and are set before the training process. Hyperparameters include learning rates, the number of layers in a neural network, and the number of clusters in clustering algorithms.

Important Concepts in AI

1. **Training and Testing**:
   - In machine learning, the dataset is typically divided into two parts: the training set and the testing set. The training set is used to train the model, while the testing set is used to evaluate the model's performance on unseen data.

2. **Overfitting and Underfitting**:
   - Overfitting occurs when a model learns the training data too well, including noise and outliers, resulting in poor generalization to new data. Underfitting occurs when a model fails to capture the underlying patterns in the data, resulting in poor performance on both the training and testing sets.

3. **Bias and Variance**:
   - Bias refers to errors introduced by approximating a real-world problem with a simplified model. Variance refers to errors introduced by the model's sensitivity to small fluctuations in the training data. Achieving a balance between bias and variance is crucial for creating effective models.

4. **Gradient Descent**:
   - An optimization algorithm used to minimize the loss function of a machine learning model by iteratively updating the model's parameters in the direction of the steepest

descent.

5. **Loss Function**:
    ◦ A function that measures the difference between the predicted output and the actual output of a model. The goal of training a model is to minimize the loss function.

6. **Activation Function**:
    ◦ A function used in neural networks to introduce non-linearity into the model, allowing it to learn complex patterns. Common activation functions include the sigmoid, tanh, and ReLU functions.

7. **Backpropagation**:
    ◦ A training algorithm used in neural networks to calculate the gradient of the loss function with respect to the model's parameters. Backpropagation is used to update the model's weights during training.

8. **Regularization**:
    ◦ Techniques used to prevent overfitting by adding a penalty to the loss function. Common regularization methods include L1 and L2 regularization and dropout.

9. **Cross-Validation**:
    ◦ A technique used to evaluate the performance of a machine learning model by dividing the data into multiple subsets and training/ testing the model on different combinations of these subsets.

10. **Dimensionality Reduction**:
    ◦ Techniques used to reduce the number of features in a dataset while preserving its important properties. Common methods

include Principal Component Analysis (PCA) and t-Distributed Stochastic Neighbor Embedding (t-SNE).

Overview of AI Techniques

1. **Symbolic AI**:
   - An approach to AI that uses symbolic representations and logic-based reasoning to solve problems. Symbolic AI was dominant in the early days of AI research but has since been supplemented by data-driven approaches.

2. **Machine Learning Algorithms**:
   - Algorithms that enable machines to learn from data and make predictions or decisions. Examples include linear regression, decision trees, support vector machines (SVM), and k-nearest neighbors (KNN).

3. **Deep Learning Algorithms**:
   - Advanced machine learning algorithms that use neural networks with multiple layers to learn from large amounts of data. Examples include CNNs, RNNs, and GANs.

4. **Reinforcement Learning Algorithms**:
   - Algorithms that enable agents to learn by interacting with their environment and receiving feedback in the form of rewards or penalties. Examples include Q-learning and Deep Q-Networks (DQNs).

5. **Natural Language Processing Techniques**:
   - Techniques used to process and understand human language. Examples include tokenization, part-of-speech tagging, named entity recognition, and sentiment analysis.

6. **Computer Vision Techniques**:

   ◦ Techniques used to analyze and interpret visual information. Examples include image classification, object detection, image segmentation, and facial recognition.

Conclusion

Familiarizing yourself with key AI terminology and concepts is essential for understanding the complexities of artificial intelligence. In this chapter, we have provided an overview of important terms and principles, including machine learning, neural networks, natural language processing, computer vision, and reinforcement learning. We have also explored fundamental concepts such as training and testing, overfitting and underfitting, bias and variance, gradient descent, and regularization.

As you continue your journey through this book, these foundational terms and concepts will serve as building blocks for more advanced topics and techniques in AI. In the next chapter, we will delve into the AI ecosystem, exploring key players, research communities, and the hardware and software that power AI advancements.

CHAPTER 5: THE AI ECOSYSTEM

Overview

The field of artificial intelligence (AI) is vast and continually evolving, supported by a robust ecosystem that includes research institutions, academic communities, commercial enterprises, and a variety of technological innovations. Understanding the AI ecosystem is crucial for appreciating the interconnected nature of AI development and the various players contributing to its progress. In this chapter, we will explore the key components of the AI ecosystem, including major players, research communities, hardware and software advancements, and the collaborative efforts driving AI innovation.

Key Players in the AI Industry

1. **Tech Giants**:

   ◦ Major technology companies, often referred to as tech giants, play a pivotal role in advancing AI research and development. These companies invest heavily in AI and contribute to both foundational research and practical applications. Notable tech giants in the AI industry include:

      ▪ **Google:** Through its AI research division, Google AI, and its acquisition of DeepMind, Google has made significant strides in areas such as machine learning, natural language processing (NLP), and computer vision.

- **Microsoft:** Microsoft AI focuses on developing AI tools, platforms, and solutions for various industries. The company also invests in AI research through Microsoft Research and partnerships with academic institutions.

- **Amazon:** Amazon AI powers many of the company's services, including Amazon Web Services (AWS), which offers a range of AI and machine learning services to developers and businesses.

- **IBM:** IBM's Watson AI platform provides AI solutions for industries such as healthcare, finance, and education. IBM Research continues to explore cutting-edge AI technologies.

- **Facebook:** Facebook AI Research (FAIR) focuses on advancing the state of AI through open research and collaboration. Facebook leverages AI for content moderation, recommendations, and more.

2. **Academic Institutions**:

    ◦ Universities and research institutions are at the forefront of AI research, contributing to theoretical advancements and practical innovations. Some of the leading academic institutions in AI research include:

        - **Stanford University:** Known for its

AI research lab and contributions to machine learning, robotics, and NLP.

- **Massachusetts Institute of Technology (MIT):** Home to the MIT Computer Science and Artificial Intelligence Laboratory (CSAIL), which conducts interdisciplinary AI research.
- **Carnegie Mellon University (CMU):** Renowned for its AI research in robotics, machine learning, and human-computer interaction.
- **University of California, Berkeley:** Hosts the Berkeley Artificial Intelligence Research (BAIR) Lab, focusing on deep learning, reinforcement learning, and robotics.

3. **Startups and Innovators:**

   ○ AI startups and innovators bring fresh ideas and novel approaches to the field. They often focus on niche applications and push the boundaries of AI technology. Some notable AI startups include:

   - **OpenAI:** A research organization dedicated to ensuring that artificial general intelligence (AGI) benefits all of humanity. OpenAI develops advanced AI models and shares its research openly.
   - **Nuro:** Specializes in autonomous delivery vehicles designed to transport goods efficiently and safely.
   - **UiPath:** A leading company in robotic process automation (RPA), providing

tools for automating repetitive business tasks using AI.

AI Research Communities

1. **Conferences and Workshops**:
   - AI research communities gather at conferences and workshops to share knowledge, present research findings, and collaborate on new projects. Some of the most prestigious AI conferences include:
     - **NeurIPS (Conference on Neural Information Processing Systems):** A premier conference on machine learning and computational neuroscience.
     - **ICML (International Conference on Machine Learning):** Focuses on advancements in machine learning algorithms, theory, and applications.
     - **CVPR (Conference on Computer Vision and Pattern Recognition):** A leading conference in the field of computer vision.
     - **AAAI (Association for the Advancement of Artificial Intelligence):** Covers a wide range of AI topics, including machine learning, robotics, and NLP.

2. **Collaborative Research Initiatives**:
   - Collaborative research initiatives bring together researchers from academia, industry, and government to work on ambitious AI projects. Examples include:
     - **Partnership on AI:** An alliance of organizations dedicated to promoting

responsible AI development and addressing ethical challenges.

- **AI4ALL:** An initiative aimed at increasing diversity and inclusion in AI by providing education and mentorship to underrepresented groups.

3. **Open Source Communities**:

   - Open source communities play a crucial role in AI by developing and sharing tools, frameworks, and datasets. Open source projects enable widespread access to AI technologies and foster collaboration. Notable open source projects include:

     - **TensorFlow:** An open source machine learning framework developed by Google, widely used for building and deploying AI models.

     - **PyTorch:** An open source deep learning framework developed by Facebook, known for its flexibility and ease of use.

     - **Hugging Face:** An open source community focused on NLP, providing pre-trained models and libraries for tasks such as text classification and language generation.

Hardware and Software Advancements

1. **AI Hardware**:

   - The development of specialized hardware accelerates AI computations and enables the training of large-scale models. Key advancements in AI hardware include:

     - **Graphics Processing Units (GPUs):**

GPUs, originally designed for rendering graphics, are now extensively used for parallel processing in AI tasks. Companies like NVIDIA lead the market in AI-optimized GPUs.

- **Tensor Processing Units (TPUs):** Custom-built by Google, TPUs are designed specifically for accelerating machine learning workloads, offering high performance and efficiency.

- **Application-Specific Integrated Circuits (ASICs):** Specialized chips optimized for specific AI applications, such as autonomous vehicles and edge computing.

2. **AI Software and Frameworks**:

    ○ AI software and frameworks provide the tools and libraries necessary for developing and deploying AI models. Key software advancements include:

        - **Deep Learning Frameworks:** TensorFlow, PyTorch, and Keras are among the most popular frameworks for building and training deep learning models.

        - **AutoML Tools:** Automated machine learning tools, such as Google's AutoML and H2O.ai, enable non-experts to build and deploy machine learning models with minimal manual intervention.

        - **NLP Libraries:** Libraries like Hugging Face's Transformers provide pre-trained models and tools for natural language processing tasks.

Collaborative Efforts in AI

1. **Industry-Academic Partnerships**:
   - Collaboration between industry and academia accelerates AI research and development by combining theoretical insights with practical applications. Examples of such partnerships include:
     - **MIT-IBM Watson AI Lab:** A collaboration between MIT and IBM focused on advancing AI research in areas such as healthcare, cybersecurity, and automation.
     - **Stanford Human-Centered AI Institute (HAI):** Supported by industry partners, HAI aims to advance AI research that prioritizes human well-being and ethical considerations.

2. **Government and Policy Initiatives**:
   - Governments and policymakers play a crucial role in shaping the AI landscape by providing funding, creating regulatory frameworks, and promoting ethical AI development. Notable initiatives include:
     - **National AI Strategies:** Countries like the United States, China, and the European Union have developed national AI strategies to guide research, investment, and policy decisions.
     - **AI Ethics Guidelines:** Organizations such as the European Commission

have published guidelines on trustworthy AI, emphasizing principles like transparency, accountability, and fairness.

3. **Global AI Challenges and Competitions**:

   ◦ AI challenges and competitions foster innovation and collaboration by encouraging researchers and practitioners to tackle complex problems. Examples include:

     ▪ **ImageNet Challenge:** A competition focused on advancing image classification and object detection techniques.

     ▪ **Kaggle Competitions:** An online platform that hosts data science and machine learning competitions, allowing participants to collaborate and compete on real-world problems.

Conclusion

The AI ecosystem is a dynamic and collaborative network of key players, research communities, hardware and software advancements, and various initiatives driving the field forward. Understanding the interconnected nature of the AI ecosystem provides valuable insights into the collaborative efforts that underpin AI innovation and development.

In this chapter, we explored the major players in the AI industry, including tech giants, academic institutions, and startups. We also examined the role of AI research communities, conferences, open source projects, and collaborative initiatives. Additionally, we discussed advancements in AI hardware and software that are accelerating progress in the field.

As we continue our journey through the subsequent chapters, we will delve deeper into specific AI techniques, technologies, and their practical applications. In the next chapter, we will explore the fundamentals of machine learning, a key component of AI that enables machines to learn from data and make predictions or decisions.

CHAPTER 6: INTRODUCTION TO MACHINE LEARNING

Overview

Machine Learning (ML) is a subset of artificial intelligence (AI) that focuses on the development of algorithms that enable computers to learn from and make predictions or decisions based on data. Machine learning is the driving force behind many of the AI applications we use today, from recommendation systems to autonomous vehicles. In this chapter, we will explore the fundamentals of machine learning, its types, and its importance. We will also discuss key concepts and provide an overview of the machine learning workflow.

Definition and Types of Machine Learning

Definition: Machine Learning is the process of teaching computers to learn patterns and make decisions without being explicitly programmed. It involves the use of statistical techniques to build models that can analyze and interpret data, recognize patterns, and make predictions or decisions.

Types of Machine Learning: Machine learning can be broadly classified into three main types:

1. **Supervised Learning:**
   - In supervised learning, the algorithm is trained on labeled data, meaning that each training example is paired with an output

label. The goal is to learn a mapping from inputs to outputs based on the labeled examples.

- **Examples:**
  - Classification: Predicting a discrete label (e.g., spam or not spam).
  - Regression: Predicting a continuous value (e.g., house prices).

2. **Unsupervised Learning:**

- In unsupervised learning, the algorithm is trained on unlabeled data, meaning that there are no output labels provided. The goal is to identify patterns and relationships within the data.
- **Examples:**
  - Clustering: Grouping similar data points together (e.g., customer segmentation).
  - Association: Discovering relationships between variables (e.g., market basket analysis).

3. **Reinforcement Learning:**

- In reinforcement learning, an agent interacts with its environment and learns by receiving feedback in the form of rewards or penalties. The goal is to learn a policy that maximizes cumulative rewards over time.
- **Examples:**
  - Game playing: Training agents to play games (e.g., chess, Go).
  - Robotics: Training robots to perform tasks (e.g., navigating obstacles).

Importance of Machine Learning

Machine learning is transforming various industries by enabling new capabilities and improving existing processes. Its importance can be summarized as follows:

1. **Automation:**
   - Machine learning automates repetitive and mundane tasks, freeing up human workers to focus on more complex and creative activities.

2. **Data-Driven Decision Making:**
   - Machine learning models can analyze vast amounts of data and provide insights and recommendations, enhancing decision-making processes.

3. **Personalization:**
   - Machine learning enables personalized experiences by tailoring content, products, and services to individual preferences and behaviors.

4. **Predictive Analytics:**
   - Machine learning models can make accurate predictions based on historical data, helping businesses anticipate future trends and outcomes.

5. **Efficiency and Accuracy:**
   - Machine learning algorithms can perform tasks with high efficiency and accuracy, often surpassing human capabilities in specific domains.

Key Concepts in Machine Learning

1. **Training and Testing:**
   - **Training Set:** The dataset used to train a machine learning model. It contains input-output pairs that the model learns from.
   - **Testing Set:** The dataset used to evaluate

the performance of the trained model on unseen data. It helps assess the model's generalization capabilities.

2. **Features and Labels:**
   - **Features:** The input variables or attributes used by the model to make predictions (e.g., age, income, education level).
   - **Labels:** The target variable or output that the model is trying to predict (e.g., whether an email is spam or not).

3. **Model Evaluation:**
   - **Accuracy:** The proportion of correctly predicted instances out of the total instances.
   - **Precision:** The proportion of true positive predictions out of all positive predictions.
   - **Recall:** The proportion of true positive predictions out of all actual positives.
   - **F1 Score:** The harmonic mean of precision and recall, providing a single metric to evaluate model performance.

4. **Overfitting and Underfitting:**
   - **Overfitting:** When a model learns the training data too well, including noise and outliers, resulting in poor generalization to new data.
   - **Underfitting:** When a model fails to capture the underlying patterns in the data, resulting in poor performance on both training and testing sets.

5. **Bias and Variance:**
   - **Bias:** The error introduced by approximating a real-world problem with a simplified model. High bias can lead to underfitting.

- ◦ **Variance:** The error introduced by the model's sensitivity to small fluctuations in the training data. High variance can lead to overfitting.

6. **Regularization:**
    - ◦ Techniques used to prevent overfitting by adding a penalty to the loss function. Common regularization methods include L1 and L2 regularization.

Machine Learning Workflow

The machine learning workflow consists of several key steps that guide the development and deployment of machine learning models:

1. **Problem Definition:**
    - ◦ Clearly define the problem you are trying to solve and identify the objectives and requirements of the machine learning model.

2. **Data Collection:**
    - ◦ Gather relevant data from various sources, ensuring that the data is representative and sufficient for training the model.

3. **Data Preprocessing:**
    - ◦ Clean and preprocess the data to remove noise, handle missing values, and transform the data into a suitable format for modeling. This step includes feature selection and extraction.

4. **Model Selection:**
    - ◦ Choose an appropriate machine learning algorithm based on the problem type, data characteristics, and desired outcomes.

5. **Model Training:**
    - ◦ Train the selected model using the training

dataset. Adjust hyperparameters and use techniques like cross-validation to optimize model performance.

6. **Model Evaluation:**

   ◦ Evaluate the trained model using the testing dataset and appropriate evaluation metrics. Assess the model's performance and identify any issues such as overfitting or underfitting.

7. **Model Deployment:**

   ◦ Deploy the trained model into a production environment where it can make predictions or decisions on new data. Ensure that the deployment process is scalable and robust.

8. **Monitoring and Maintenance:**

   ◦ Continuously monitor the deployed model's performance and make necessary updates or retraining as new data becomes available. Address any issues that arise and ensure the model remains accurate and relevant.

Conclusion

Machine learning is a powerful subset of artificial intelligence that enables computers to learn from data and make predictions or decisions. In this chapter, we explored the definition and types of machine learning, including supervised learning, unsupervised learning, and reinforcement learning. We also discussed the importance of machine learning and key concepts such as training and testing, features and labels, model evaluation, overfitting and underfitting, and bias and variance.

Understanding the machine learning workflow, from problem definition to model deployment and maintenance, provides a comprehensive framework for developing and implementing machine learning models. As we continue our journey through the subsequent chapters, we will delve deeper into specific machine learning algorithms, techniques, and practical applications.

In the next chapter, we will explore data preprocessing, a crucial step in the machine learning workflow that ensures the data is clean, relevant, and ready for modeling.

CHAPTER 7: DATA PREPROCESSING

Overview

Data preprocessing is a crucial step in the machine learning workflow. It involves preparing raw data for analysis by cleaning, transforming, and organizing it into a suitable format for modeling. Effective data preprocessing ensures that the data used for training machine learning models is accurate, relevant, and of high quality, ultimately leading to better model performance. In this chapter, we will explore the importance of data preprocessing, key techniques, and best practices for preparing data for machine learning.

Importance of Data Preprocessing

1. **Improved Data Quality**:
   - Raw data often contains noise, missing values, and inconsistencies that can negatively impact model performance. Data preprocessing helps improve the quality of the data by addressing these issues.

2. **Enhanced Model Performance**:
   - Clean and well-prepared data enables machine learning models to learn patterns more effectively, leading to better predictions and decisions. Proper data preprocessing can reduce overfitting and improve generalization.

3. **Efficient Computation**:

- Data preprocessing can reduce the size and complexity of the dataset, making it easier to process and analyze. This leads to faster model training and evaluation times.

4. **Accurate Feature Representation:**

- Transforming raw data into meaningful features helps machine learning models understand and interpret the data better. Feature engineering is a key aspect of data preprocessing that enhances model accuracy.

Key Steps in Data Preprocessing

1. **Data Collection:**

- The first step in data preprocessing is collecting relevant data from various sources, such as databases, APIs, web scraping, and sensors. It is essential to ensure that the collected data is representative of the problem being addressed.

2. **Data Cleaning:**

- Data cleaning involves identifying and addressing issues such as missing values, noise, and outliers. Key techniques for data cleaning include:

  - **Handling Missing Values:** Strategies for handling missing data include imputation (e.g., filling missing values with the mean or median) and removal of rows or columns with missing values.

  - **Removing Noise:** Noise in data refers to random errors or irrelevant information. Techniques for noise removal include smoothing, filtering, and aggregation.

- **Outlier Detection:** Outliers are data points that deviate significantly from the rest of the data. Outlier detection methods include statistical tests, clustering, and visual inspection.

3. **Data Transformation:**

   ○ Data transformation involves converting raw data into a format suitable for modeling. Key techniques for data transformation include:

     - **Normalization and Scaling:** Normalization (scaling data to a range of [0, 1]) and standardization (scaling data to have a mean of 0 and standard deviation of 1) ensure that features are on a similar scale.

     - **Encoding Categorical Variables:** Converting categorical variables into numerical representations using techniques such as one-hot encoding and label encoding.

     - **Feature Engineering:** Creating new features from existing data to improve model performance. Techniques include polynomial features, interaction terms, and domain-specific feature creation.

4. **Data Integration:**

   ○ Data integration involves combining data from multiple sources to create a unified dataset. This may include merging datasets, handling duplicate records, and resolving inconsistencies.

5. **Feature Selection:**

   ○ Feature selection is the process of identifying

the most relevant features for modeling. Techniques for feature selection include:

- **Filter Methods:** Selecting features based on statistical measures such as correlation, chi-square, and mutual information.
- **Wrapper Methods:** Using model performance metrics to evaluate and select feature subsets (e.g., recursive feature elimination).
- **Embedded Methods:** Integrating feature selection within the model training process (e.g., Lasso regression, decision tree feature importance).

6. **Dimensionality Reduction**:

   - Dimensionality reduction techniques reduce the number of features while preserving important information. Common methods include:

     - **Principal Component Analysis (PCA):** Transforming features into a lower-dimensional space while retaining maximum variance.
     - **t-Distributed Stochastic Neighbor Embedding (t-SNE):** Visualizing high-dimensional data in a lower-dimensional space for exploration and analysis.

7. **Data Splitting**:

   - Splitting the dataset into training, validation, and testing sets to evaluate model performance and prevent overfitting. Common splits include:

- **Training Set:** Used to train the model.
- **Validation Set:** Used to tune hyperparameters and select the best model.
- **Testing Set:** Used to evaluate the final model's performance on unseen data.

Best Practices for Data Preprocessing

1. **Understand the Data:**
   - Before preprocessing, thoroughly explore and understand the data, including its structure, distribution, and key characteristics. Use visualizations and descriptive statistics to gain insights into the data.

2. **Document the Process:**
   - Document each step of the data preprocessing process, including the rationale for decisions made and any transformations applied. This ensures transparency and reproducibility.

3. **Iterative Approach:**
   - Data preprocessing is often an iterative process. Continuously refine and adjust preprocessing techniques based on feedback from model performance and domain knowledge.

4. **Data Quality Checks:**
   - Perform data quality checks at each stage of preprocessing to ensure that the data remains accurate and consistent. This includes checking for missing values, duplicates, and inconsistencies.

5. **Automate When Possible:**
   - Automate repetitive and time-consuming preprocessing tasks using scripts and tools.

This increases efficiency and reduces the likelihood of errors.

6. **Keep Raw Data Intact**:
   - Always retain a copy of the raw data in its original form. This allows for reprocessing if needed and ensures that no valuable information is lost.

7. **Collaborate with Domain Experts**:
   - Collaborate with domain experts to gain insights into the data and ensure that preprocessing techniques are appropriate and relevant for the specific problem.

Conclusion

Data preprocessing is a critical step in the machine learning workflow that ensures the data used for modeling is accurate, relevant, and of high quality. In this chapter, we explored the importance of data preprocessing and key techniques, including data cleaning, transformation, integration, feature selection, and dimensionality reduction. We also discussed best practices for effective data preprocessing, such as understanding the data, documenting the process, and collaborating with domain experts.

By following these principles and techniques, you can prepare your data effectively, leading to improved model performance and more accurate predictions. As we continue our journey through the subsequent chapters, we will delve deeper into specific machine learning algorithms and their practical applications.

In the next chapter, we will explore supervised learning algorithms, including linear regression, logistic regression, decision trees, and support vector machines (SVM). We will examine how these algorithms work, their strengths and limitations, and practical use cases.

CHAPTER 8: SUPERVISED LEARNING ALGORITHMS

Overview

Supervised learning is a type of machine learning where the model is trained on labeled data. In supervised learning, each training example consists of an input and a corresponding output label. The goal of supervised learning is to learn a mapping from inputs to outputs based on the labeled data, allowing the model to make predictions on new, unseen data. This chapter delves into several key supervised learning algorithms, including linear regression, logistic regression, decision trees, and support vector machines (SVM). We will explore how these algorithms work, their strengths and limitations, and practical use cases.

Linear Regression

Definition: Linear regression is a statistical method used to model the relationship between a dependent variable (target) and one or more independent variables (features). It assumes a linear relationship between the variables and aims to find the best-fitting line that minimizes the sum of squared differences between the observed and predicted values.

How It Works:

- **Simple Linear Regression:** In simple linear regression, the model predicts the target variable using a single feature. The relationship is modeled by the equation: $y = b_0 + b_1x$, where y is the predicted value, x is the feature, b_0 is the intercept, and b_1 is the slope.

- **Multiple Linear Regression:** In multiple linear regression, the model uses multiple features to predict the target variable. The relationship is modeled by the equation: $y = b_0 + b_1x_1 + b_2x_2 + \ldots + b_nx_n$, where $x_1, x_2, \ldots, x_n$ are the features and $b_1, b_2, \ldots, b_n$ are the coefficients.

Strengths:

- Simple and easy to interpret.
- Computationally efficient.
- Works well with linearly separable data.

Limitations:

- Assumes a linear relationship between features and the target.
- Sensitive to outliers.
- May not perform well with complex or non-linear data.

Use Cases:

- Predicting house prices based on features such as square footage, number of bedrooms, and location.
- Estimating sales revenue based on advertising spend and marketing efforts.

Logistic Regression

Definition: Logistic regression is a classification algorithm used to model the probability of a binary outcome (e.g., success/failure, yes/no) based on one or more features. It uses the logistic function (sigmoid function) to map predicted values to probabilities.

How It Works:

- The model predicts the probability that the target variable belongs to a particular class. The relationship is modeled by the equation:
  logit(p)=ln(p1-p)=b0+b1x1+b2x2+...+bnxn
  $\text{logit}(p) = \ln\left(\frac{p}{1-p}\right) = b_0 + b_1x_1 + b_2x_2 + \ldots + b_nx_n$, where p is the probability of the positive class, $x1,x2,...,xn$ $x_1, x_2, \ldots, x_n$ are the features, and b0,b1,...,bn $b_0, b_1, \ldots, b_n$ are the coefficients.

- The logistic function (sigmoid function) is used to convert the logit (linear combination of features) to a probability: p=11+e-logit(p) $p = \frac{1}{1 + e^{-\text{logit}(p)}}$.

Strengths:

- Effective for binary classification problems.
- Provides probabilities for class membership.
- Easy to implement and interpret.

Limitations:

- Assumes a linear relationship between features and the logit of the target.
- May not perform well with non-linear data or when classes are not well separated.
- Sensitive to outliers.

Use Cases:

- Predicting whether a customer will purchase a product based on features such as age, income, and browsing behavior.
- Classifying emails as spam or not spam based on the content and sender information.

Decision Trees

Definition: Decision trees are a non-linear supervised learning algorithm used for both classification and regression tasks. They work by recursively splitting the data into subsets based on feature values, resulting in a tree-like structure where each node represents a feature and each branch represents a decision.

How It Works:

- The tree is built by selecting the best feature to split the data at each node, based on criteria such as information gain (for classification) or mean squared error reduction (for regression).
- The process continues recursively until a stopping criterion is met, such as a maximum tree depth or a minimum number of samples per leaf.
- The final model consists of decision nodes and leaf nodes, where each leaf node represents a predicted outcome.

Strengths:

- Easy to interpret and visualize.
- Handles both numerical and categorical data.
- Captures non-linear relationships.

Limitations:

- Prone to overfitting, especially with deep trees.
- Sensitive to small changes in the data.
- Can be biased towards features with many levels.

Use Cases:

- Classifying customers into different segments based on demographic and behavioral features.
- Predicting loan default risk based on features such as credit score, income, and loan amount.

Support Vector Machines (SVM)

Definition: Support Vector Machines (SVM) are a supervised learning algorithm used for classification and regression tasks.

SVM aims to find the hyperplane that best separates the data into classes while maximizing the margin between the closest data points (support vectors) and the hyperplane.

How It Works:

- The algorithm identifies the hyperplane that maximizes the margin between the support vectors of different classes.
- For non-linearly separable data, SVM uses kernel functions (e.g., linear, polynomial, radial basis function) to transform the data into a higher-dimensional space where a linear hyperplane can be found.
- The decision boundary is defined by the support vectors, and the model aims to minimize the classification error.

Strengths:

- Effective for high-dimensional data.
- Robust to overfitting, especially with appropriate regularization.
- Can handle non-linear relationships with kernel functions.

Limitations:

- Computationally intensive, especially with large datasets.
- Choosing the right kernel and hyperparameters can be challenging.
- Less interpretable compared to simpler models.

Use Cases:

- Classifying images of handwritten digits based on pixel values.
- Detecting fraudulent transactions based on transaction features and patterns.

Conclusion

Supervised learning algorithms are essential tools in the machine learning toolbox, enabling the development of models that can make accurate predictions based on labeled data. In this chapter, we explored several key supervised learning algorithms, including linear regression, logistic regression, decision trees, and support vector machines (SVM). We discussed how these algorithms work, their strengths and limitations, and practical use cases.

By understanding the principles and applications of these supervised learning algorithms, you can select the most appropriate model for your specific problem and achieve better predictive performance. As we continue our journey through the subsequent chapters, we will delve deeper into unsupervised learning algorithms and their practical applications.

In the next chapter, we will explore unsupervised learning algorithms, including clustering, association rule learning, and dimensionality reduction techniques. We will examine how these algorithms work, their strengths and limitations, and practical use cases.

CHAPTER 9: UNSUPERVISED LEARNING ALGORITHMS

Overview

Unsupervised learning is a type of machine learning where the model is trained on unlabeled data. Unlike supervised learning, there are no explicit output labels provided. Instead, the goal of unsupervised learning is to identify patterns, structures, or relationships within the data. This chapter delves into several key unsupervised learning algorithms, including clustering, association rule learning, and dimensionality reduction techniques. We will explore how these algorithms work, their strengths and limitations, and practical use cases.

Clustering Algorithms

Definition: Clustering is a type of unsupervised learning that involves grouping similar data points together into clusters. The objective is to maximize the similarity within each cluster and minimize the similarity between different clusters.

Key Clustering Algorithms:

1. **K-Means Clustering:**

   - **How It Works:** K-means clustering partitions the data into kk clusters, where kk is a predefined number. The algorithm iteratively assigns data points to clusters based on their proximity to the cluster centroids and updates the centroids based on the mean of the assigned points.

- **Strengths:** Simple and efficient; works well with large datasets.
- **Limitations:** Requires the number of clusters to be specified in advance; sensitive to the initial placement of centroids; may not perform well with non-spherical clusters.
- **Use Cases:** Customer segmentation, document clustering, image compression.

2. **Hierarchical Clustering:**

- **How It Works:** Hierarchical clustering builds a tree-like structure of nested clusters. It can be agglomerative (bottom-up) or divisive (top-down). In agglomerative clustering, each data point starts as its own cluster, and clusters are recursively merged based on similarity. In divisive clustering, the entire dataset starts as one cluster, and clusters are recursively split.
- **Strengths:** Does not require the number of clusters to be specified in advance; produces a dendrogram that visualizes the cluster hierarchy.
- **Limitations:** Computationally intensive with large datasets; sensitive to noise and outliers.
- **Use Cases:** Gene expression analysis, social network analysis, customer behavior analysis.

3. **DBSCAN (Density-Based Spatial Clustering of Applications with Noise):**

- **How It Works:** DBSCAN identifies clusters based on the density of data points in the feature space. It defines clusters as dense regions separated by sparse regions. The algorithm requires two parameters: the radius of the neighborhood (ϵ\epsilon) and the minimum number of points required to form a dense region (minPts).

- **Strengths:** Does not require the number of clusters to be specified in advance; can identify arbitrarily shaped clusters; robust to noise and outliers.
- **Limitations:** Sensitive to parameter selection (ϵ\epsilon and minPts); may struggle with varying density clusters.
- **Use Cases:** Anomaly detection, spatial data analysis, market basket analysis.

Association Rule Learning

Definition: Association rule learning is a type of unsupervised learning that identifies interesting associations or relationships between variables in large datasets. It is commonly used in market basket analysis to discover patterns in transactional data.

Key Association Rule Learning Algorithms:

1. **Apriori Algorithm:**
    - **How It Works:** The Apriori algorithm generates frequent itemsets by iteratively expanding smaller itemsets that meet a minimum support threshold. It then derives association rules from these frequent itemsets based on a minimum confidence threshold.
    - **Strengths:** Simple and easy to implement; effective for small to medium-sized datasets.
    - **Limitations:** Computationally intensive with large datasets; may generate a large number of candidate itemsets.

    ◦ **Use Cases:** Market basket analysis, product recommendation, cross-selling strategies.

2. **Eclat Algorithm:**

    ◦ **How It Works:** The Eclat algorithm is an improvement over the Apriori algorithm that uses a depth-first search strategy to generate frequent itemsets. It represents itemsets as vertical bitmaps, reducing the need for multiple scans of the dataset.

    ◦ **Strengths:** More efficient than the Apriori algorithm for large datasets; reduces the number of database scans.

    ◦ **Limitations:** Requires more memory to store vertical bitmaps; may struggle with very large itemsets.

    ◦ **Use Cases:** Market basket analysis, association rule mining, text mining.

Dimensionality Reduction Techniques

Definition: Dimensionality reduction techniques reduce the number of features in a dataset while preserving its important properties. These techniques are used to simplify data, remove noise, and improve computational efficiency.

Key Dimensionality Reduction Techniques:

1. **Principal Component Analysis (PCA):**

    ◦ **How It Works:** PCA transforms the data into a new coordinate system where the axes (principal components) are orthogonal and ordered by the amount of variance they capture. The first principal component captures the most variance, followed by the second, and so on.

    ◦ **Strengths:** Reduces dimensionality while preserving most of the variance; helps visualize high-dimensional data.

- **Limitations:** Assumes linear relationships between features; may lose interpretability of original features.
- **Use Cases:** Data visualization, noise reduction, feature extraction.

2. **t-Distributed Stochastic Neighbor Embedding (t-SNE):**

- **How It Works:** t-SNE is a non-linear dimensionality reduction technique that maps high-dimensional data to a lower-dimensional space by minimizing the divergence between probability distributions of pairwise distances in the original and reduced spaces.
- **Strengths:** Effective for visualizing high-dimensional data; captures non-linear relationships.
- **Limitations:** Computationally intensive; may struggle with very large datasets; not suitable for feature extraction.
- **Use Cases:** Data exploration, clustering visualization, anomaly detection.

3. **Autoencoders:**

- **How It Works:** Autoencoders are neural networks that learn to encode input data into a lower-dimensional representation and then decode it back to the original input. The encoder compresses the data, and the decoder reconstructs it, with the objective of minimizing reconstruction error.
- **Strengths:** Can capture non-linear relationships; flexible and customizable architecture.

- **Limitations:** Requires careful tuning of the network architecture and hyperparameters; may require large amounts of data.
- **Use Cases:** Data compression, noise reduction, anomaly detection.

Conclusion

Unsupervised learning algorithms play a crucial role in identifying patterns, structures, and relationships within unlabeled data. In this chapter, we explored several key unsupervised learning algorithms, including clustering algorithms (K-means, hierarchical clustering, DBSCAN), association rule learning algorithms (Apriori, Eclat), and dimensionality reduction techniques (PCA, t-SNE, autoencoders). We discussed how these algorithms work, their strengths and limitations, and practical use cases.

By understanding the principles and applications of these unsupervised learning algorithms, you can uncover valuable insights from your data and leverage them to inform decision-making and enhance various processes. As we continue our journey through the subsequent chapters, we will delve deeper into more advanced AI topics and their practical applications.

In the next chapter, we will explore evaluation metrics and model validation techniques, which are essential for assessing the performance of machine learning models and ensuring their reliability and generalization.

CHAPTER 10: EVALUATION METRICS AND MODEL VALIDATION

Overview

Evaluating the performance of machine learning models is crucial to ensure that they accurately predict or classify data, generalize well to unseen data, and provide reliable results. This chapter explores various evaluation metrics and model validation techniques used to assess the performance of machine learning models. Understanding these metrics and techniques helps practitioners select the best models and avoid common pitfalls such as overfitting and underfitting.

Evaluation Metrics

1. **Classification Metrics**:
   - Classification metrics are used to evaluate models that predict categorical outcomes. Common classification metrics include:

   Accuracy:
   - **Definition:** The proportion of correctly predicted instances out of the total instances.
   - **Formula:** Accuracy=True Positives +True NegativesTotal Instances\text{Accuracy} = \frac{\text{True Positives} + \text{True

Negatives}}{\text{Total Instances}}

- **Use Cases:** Appropriate for balanced datasets where each class is equally important.

Precision:

- **Definition:** The proportion of true positive predictions out of all positive predictions.
- **Formula:** Precision=True PositivesTrue Positives +False Positives\text{Precision} = \frac{\text{True Positives}}{\text{True Positives} + \text{False Positives}}
- **Use Cases:** Important when the cost of false positives is high, such as in spam detection.

Recall (Sensitivity):

- **Definition:** The proportion of true positive predictions out of all actual positives.
- **Formula:** Recall=True PositivesTrue Positives +False Negatives\text{Recall} = \frac{\text{True Positives}}{\text{True Positives} + \text{False Negatives}}
- **Use Cases:** Important when the cost of false negatives is high, such as in medical diagnosis.

F1 Score:

- **Definition:** The harmonic mean of precision and recall, providing a single metric to evaluate model performance.
- **Formula:** F1 Score=2×Precision×RecallPrecision +Recall\text{F1 Score} = 2 \times \frac{\text{Precision} \times \text{Recall}}{\text{Precision} + \text{Recall}}
- **Use Cases:** Useful when both precision and recall are important and need to be balanced.

Confusion Matrix:

- **Definition:** A matrix that summarizes the performance of a classification model by showing the counts of true positives, true negatives, false positives, and false negatives.
- **Use Cases:** Provides a detailed breakdown of classification performance and helps identify specific types of errors.

Area Under the ROC Curve (AUC-ROC):

- **Definition:** A metric that measures the performance of a binary classifier by plotting the true positive rate against the false positive rate at various threshold settings.
- **Use Cases:** Useful for evaluating models when class distribution is imbalanced. Higher AUC indicates better model performance.

2. Regression Metrics:

- Regression metrics are used to evaluate models that predict continuous outcomes. Common regression metrics include:

Mean Absolute Error (MAE):

- **Definition:** The average absolute difference between the predicted values and the actual values.
- **Formula:** $\text{MAE} = \frac{1}{n} \sum_{i=1}^{n} |y_i - \hat{y}_i|$
- **Use Cases:** Provides an intuitive measure of average prediction error.

Mean Squared Error (MSE):

- **Definition:** The average squared difference between the predicted values and the actual values.
- **Formula:** $\text{MSE} = \frac{1}{n} \sum_{i=1}^{n} (y_i - \hat{y}_i)^2$

- **Use Cases:** Penalizes larger errors more heavily, useful when large errors are particularly undesirable.

Root Mean Squared Error (RMSE):

- **Definition:** The square root of the mean squared error, providing an error measure in the same units as the target variable.
- **Formula:** $\text{RMSE} = \sqrt{\frac{1}{n} \sum_{i=1}^{n} (y_i - \hat{y}_i)^2}$
- **Use Cases:** Similar to MSE but more interpretable due to the same units as the target variable.

R-squared (Coefficient of Determination):

- **Definition:** A measure of how well the predicted values explain the variance in the actual values.
- **Formula:** $R^2 = 1 - \frac{\sum_{i=1}^{n} (y_i - \hat{y}_i)^2}{\sum_{i=1}^{n} (y_i - \bar{y})^2}$
- **Use Cases:** Indicates the proportion of variance explained by the model. Values range from 0 to 1, with higher values indicating better fit.

Model Validation Techniques

1. **Holdout Validation:**

   - **Definition:** A simple validation technique where the dataset is split into two parts: a training set and a testing set. The model is trained on the training set and evaluated on the testing set.
   - **Advantages:** Simple and easy to implement.
   - **Limitations:** Performance can vary depending on the random split of the data. May not be representative for small datasets.

2. **K-Fold Cross-Validation:**

- **Definition:** A validation technique that divides the dataset into k subsets (folds). The model is trained and evaluated k times, each time using a different fold as the testing set and the remaining folds as the training set. The results are averaged to obtain the final performance metric.
- **Advantages:** Provides a more reliable estimate of model performance by averaging results over multiple folds.
- **Limitations:** Computationally intensive, especially with large datasets.

3. **Leave-One-Out Cross-Validation (LOOCV):**

- **Definition:** A special case of k-fold cross-validation where k is equal to the number of instances in the dataset. Each instance is used as the testing set exactly once, and the model is trained on the remaining instances.
- **Advantages:** Utilizes the maximum amount of data for training in each iteration.
- **Limitations:** Extremely computationally intensive, especially for large datasets.

4. **Stratified K-Fold Cross-Validation:**

- **Definition:** A variant of k-fold cross-validation that ensures each fold has a similar distribution of classes (for classification tasks). This helps maintain class balance across folds.
- **Advantages:** Reduces the risk of biased performance estimates due to class imbalance.
- **Limitations:** Computationally intensive, similar to k-fold cross-validation.

5. **Repeated Cross-Validation**:
   - **Definition:** A validation technique that repeats k-fold cross-validation multiple times with different random splits of the data. The results are averaged to obtain the final performance metric.
   - **Advantages:** Provides a more robust estimate of model performance by reducing variance due to random splits.
   - **Limitations:** Even more computationally intensive than k-fold cross-validation.

6. **Bootstrap Sampling**:
   - **Definition:** A validation technique that involves repeatedly sampling (with replacement) subsets of the dataset to create multiple training sets. The model is trained on each subset and evaluated on the remaining instances. The results are averaged to obtain the final performance metric.
   - **Advantages:** Provides a robust estimate of model performance and can be used with small datasets.
   - **Limitations:** Computationally intensive and may introduce bias due to repeated sampling.

Addressing Overfitting and Underfitting

1. **Overfitting**:
   - **Definition:** Overfitting occurs when a model learns the training data too well, including noise and outliers, resulting in poor generalization to new data.
   - **Symptoms:** High accuracy on the training set but low accuracy on the testing set.
   - **Solutions:**

- **Regularization:** Techniques such as L1 and L2 regularization add a penalty to the loss function, discouraging overly complex models.
- **Pruning:** For decision trees, pruning removes branches that do not contribute significantly to the model's performance.
- **Early Stopping:** In iterative algorithms, early stopping halts training when performance on a validation set starts to degrade.
- **Cross-Validation:** Using cross-validation helps ensure the model generalizes well to new data.

2. **Underfitting:**

  ○ **Definition:** Underfitting occurs when a model fails to capture the underlying patterns in the data, resulting in poor performance on both the training and testing sets.

  ○ **Symptoms:** Low accuracy on both the training set and the testing set.

  ○ **Solutions:**

    - **Increasing Model Complexity:** Using more complex models (e.g., deeper neural networks, more trees in an ensemble) can help capture underlying patterns.
    - **Feature Engineering:** Creating new features or transforming existing ones can help improve model performance.
    - **Reducing Regularization:** Reducing the strength of regularization can allow the model to fit the training data

better.

- **Gathering More Data:** Increasing the size of the training dataset can help the model learn more effectively.

Conclusion

Evaluating machine learning models is a critical step in ensuring their accuracy, reliability, and generalization to new data. In this chapter, we explored various evaluation metrics for classification and regression tasks, including accuracy, precision, recall, F1 score, mean absolute error, mean squared error, and R-squared. We also discussed model validation techniques, such as holdout validation, k-fold cross-validation, and bootstrap sampling, which are essential for assessing model performance.

Understanding these evaluation metrics and validation techniques helps practitioners select the best models, avoid overfitting and underfitting

CHAPTER 11: INTRODUCTION TO NEURAL NETWORKS

Overview

Neural networks are a fundamental component of modern artificial intelligence (AI) and machine learning. Inspired by the structure and function of the human brain, neural networks are designed to recognize patterns, learn from data, and make predictions or decisions. In this chapter, we will explore the basics of neural networks, their architecture, key concepts such as activation functions and backpropagation, and the process of training a neural network. By understanding these principles, you will gain insights into how neural networks power many AI applications, from image recognition to natural language processing.

Structure of a Neural Network

Definition: A neural network is a computational model composed of interconnected layers of nodes (neurons) that process and transmit information. The network consists of an input layer, one or more hidden layers, and an output layer.

Components:

1. **Neurons (Nodes):**
   - Neurons are the fundamental units of a neural network. Each neuron receives inputs, processes them, and produces an output. The

output is passed to the neurons in the next layer.

2. **Layers:**

   ◦ **Input Layer:** The input layer receives the raw data and passes it to the hidden layers. The number of neurons in the input layer corresponds to the number of features in the data.

   ◦ **Hidden Layers:** Hidden layers perform computations and extract features from the input data. A neural network can have multiple hidden layers, allowing it to learn complex patterns.

   ◦ **Output Layer:** The output layer produces the final output of the network. The number of neurons in the output layer depends on the type of task (e.g., classification, regression).

3. **Weights:**

   ◦ Weights are parameters that connect neurons between layers. Each connection has an associated weight that determines the strength and direction of the signal transmitted.

4. **Biases:**

   ◦ Biases are additional parameters that allow the network to shift the activation function, providing more flexibility in learning.

Activation Functions

Definition: Activation functions introduce non-linearity into the neural network, enabling it to learn and model complex patterns. Without activation functions, a neural network would behave like a linear model.

Common Activation Functions:

1. **Sigmoid Function:**
   - **Equation:** $\sigma(x) = \frac{1}{1 + e^{-x}}$
   - **Range:** (0, 1)
   - **Use Cases:** Binary classification tasks, output layer of binary classifiers.

2. **Hyperbolic Tangent (Tanh) Function:**
   - **Equation:** $\tanh(x) = \frac{e^x - e^{-x}}{e^x + e^{-x}}$
   - **Range:** (-1, 1)
   - **Use Cases:** Hidden layers of neural networks, helps center the data around zero.

3. **Rectified Linear Unit (ReLU) Function:**
   - **Equation:** $\text{ReLU}(x) = \max(0, x)$
   - **Range:** $[0, \infty)$
   - **Use Cases:** Hidden layers of deep neural networks, helps mitigate the vanishing gradient problem.

4. **Softmax Function:**
   - **Equation:** $\text{Softmax}(z_i) = \frac{e^{z_i}}{\sum_{j=1}^{n} e^{z_j}}$
   - **Range:** (0, 1), sums to 1 across output neurons.
   - **Use Cases:** Output layer of multi-class classification tasks, produces probabilities.

Forward and Backward Propagation

Forward Propagation:

- Forward propagation is the process of passing input data through the neural network to obtain the final output. Each neuron's output is calculated by applying the activation function to the weighted sum of its inputs and bias.

- **Steps:**
    1. Initialize the input layer with the raw data.
    2. For each hidden layer, calculate the output of each neuron: $z=\sum_{i=1}^{n} w_i \cdot x_i + b$ = \sum_{i=1}^{n} w_i \cdot x_i + b, where w_iw_i are the weights, x_ix_i are the inputs, and bb is the bias.
    3. Apply the activation function to $z$zz: $a=\text{Activation}(z)$a = \text{Activation}(z).
    4. Pass the output of the hidden layer to the next layer.
    5. Repeat the process until the output layer produces the final output.

Backward Propagation (Backpropagation):

- Backpropagation is the process of adjusting the weights and biases of the neural network based on the error between the predicted output and the actual target. It uses gradient descent to minimize the loss function.

- **Steps:**
    1. Calculate the error at the output layer: $\delta=\hat{y}-y$\delta = \hat{y} - y, where $\hat{y}$y^\hat{y} is the predicted output and $y$yy is the actual target.
    2. For each layer, starting from the output layer and moving backward, compute the gradient of the loss function with respect to the weights and biases.
    3. Update the weights and biases using the gradients: $w=w-\eta \cdot \frac{\partial L}{\partial w}$w = w - \eta \cdot \frac{\partial L}{\partial w}, where η\eta is the learning rate and $\frac{\partial L}{\partial w}$∂L∂w\frac{\partial L}

{\partial w} is the gradient of the loss function.

4. Repeat the process for a specified number of iterations (epochs) or until the loss function converges.

Training a Neural Network

Steps in Training:

1. **Data Preparation:**
   - Collect and preprocess the data, including normalization, encoding categorical variables, and splitting into training and testing sets.

2. **Model Initialization:**
   - Initialize the neural network architecture, including the number of layers, number of neurons in each layer, activation functions, and initial weights and biases.

3. **Forward Propagation:**
   - Perform forward propagation to obtain the predicted output for the training data.

4. **Loss Calculation:**
   - Calculate the loss using a loss function (e.g., mean squared error, cross-entropy) that quantifies the difference between the predicted output and the actual target.

5. **Backward Propagation:**
   - Perform backward propagation to calculate gradients and update the weights and biases.

6. **Iteration:**
   - Repeat forward and backward propagation for multiple epochs until the loss function converges.

7. Model Evaluation:

- Evaluate the trained model using the testing data and appropriate evaluation metrics (e.g., accuracy, precision, recall).

Common Challenges in Training Neural Networks

1. Vanishing Gradient Problem:

- In deep neural networks, gradients can become very small during backpropagation, leading to slow learning or no learning at all. Activation functions like ReLU help mitigate this issue.

2. Overfitting:

- Overfitting occurs when the model learns the training data too well, including noise and outliers. Techniques like dropout, regularization, and early stopping can help prevent overfitting.

3. Underfitting:

- Underfitting occurs when the model fails to capture the underlying patterns in the data. Increasing model complexity, adding more hidden layers, and feature engineering can help address underfitting.

4. Choosing Hyperparameters:

- Selecting appropriate hyperparameters (e.g., learning rate, number of layers, batch size) is crucial for training neural networks effectively. Hyperparameter tuning techniques, such as grid search and random search, can help find the optimal values.

Conclusion

Neural networks are a powerful tool in the field of artificial intelligence, enabling the development of models that can recognize patterns, learn from data, and make predictions or decisions. In this chapter, we explored the structure of neural networks, key components such as neurons and layers, activation functions, and the processes of forward and backward propagation. We also discussed the steps involved in training a neural network and common challenges that practitioners may encounter.

By understanding these fundamental concepts, you can build and train neural networks for various AI applications, from image recognition to natural language processing. As we continue our journey through the subsequent chapters, we will delve deeper into more advanced neural network architectures and their practical applications.

In the next chapter, we will explore deep learning basics, including the importance of big data and computing power, and common deep learning frameworks. We will also discuss the key differences between deep learning and traditional machine learning.

CHAPTER 12: DEEP LEARNING BASICS

Overview

Deep learning is a subset of machine learning that uses neural networks with multiple layers (hence the term "deep") to learn from large amounts of data and make complex decisions. It has gained significant attention and success in various applications such as image and speech recognition, natural language processing, and autonomous driving. This chapter explores the fundamentals of deep learning, the importance of big data and computing power, common deep learning frameworks, and key differences between deep learning and traditional machine learning.

Importance of Deep Learning

Deep learning has become a powerful tool in the field of artificial intelligence due to its ability to:

1. **Handle Large and Complex Datasets**: Deep learning models can process vast amounts of data and learn intricate patterns and representations, making them suitable for complex tasks.

2. **Achieve High Accuracy**: Deep learning models, especially deep neural networks, have achieved state-of-the-art performance in various tasks, often surpassing traditional machine learning models.

3. **Automate Feature Extraction**: Deep learning models can automatically learn and extract relevant features from raw data, reducing the need for manual feature

engineering.

4. **Generalize Well to New Data**: Properly trained deep learning models can generalize well to new, unseen data, making them effective for real-world applications.

The Role of Big Data and Computing Power

Big Data:

- Deep learning thrives on large datasets, as the models require substantial amounts of data to learn meaningful patterns and representations. Big data provides the diversity and volume needed to train deep neural networks effectively.

- The availability of big data from sources such as social media, sensors, and the internet has fueled the growth of deep learning applications.

Computing Power:

- Deep learning models are computationally intensive and require significant processing power for training and inference. Advances in hardware, particularly Graphics Processing Units (GPUs) and Tensor Processing Units (TPUs), have made it possible to train deep learning models efficiently.

- GPUs are well-suited for parallel processing, which accelerates the training of deep neural networks. TPUs, developed by Google, are specialized hardware designed specifically for deep learning tasks.

Common Deep Learning Frameworks

Several deep learning frameworks provide tools and libraries for building, training, and deploying deep neural networks. These frameworks simplify the development process and offer support for various deep learning architectures. Some of the most popular deep learning frameworks include:

1. **TensorFlow:**

- Developed by Google, TensorFlow is an open-source deep learning framework widely used for building and deploying machine learning models. It supports a variety of neural network architectures and provides tools for both research and production.

2. **PyTorch**:

- Developed by Facebook's AI Research (FAIR) lab, PyTorch is an open-source deep learning framework known for its flexibility and ease of use. It is particularly popular in the research community and supports dynamic computation graphs, making it suitable for experimentation.

3. **Keras**:

- Keras is an open-source deep learning library that provides a high-level interface for building and training neural networks. It is user-friendly and can run on top of other frameworks such as TensorFlow and Theano.

4. **Microsoft Cognitive Toolkit (CNTK)**:

- Developed by Microsoft, CNTK is an open-source deep learning framework designed for training large-scale neural networks. It offers efficient and scalable solutions for various deep learning tasks.

5. **Caffe**:

- Developed by the Berkeley Vision and Learning Center (BVLC), Caffe is an open-source deep learning framework optimized for speed and modularity. It is widely used in computer vision applications.

Key Differences Between Deep Learning and Traditional Machine Learning

1. **Feature Engineering**:
   - **Traditional Machine Learning**: Requires manual feature engineering, where domain experts design and extract relevant features from raw data.
   - **Deep Learning**: Automatically learns and extracts features from raw data through multiple layers of the network, reducing the need for manual feature engineering.

2. **Model Complexity**:
   - **Traditional Machine Learning**: Typically uses simpler models such as linear regression, decision trees, and support vector machines, which may struggle with complex patterns and high-dimensional data.
   - **Deep Learning**: Uses deep neural networks with many layers, allowing them to learn complex patterns and representations in high-dimensional data.

3. **Data Requirements**:
   - **Traditional Machine Learning**: Can work with smaller datasets, although performance may be limited.
   - **Deep Learning**: Requires large datasets to achieve high performance and generalize well to new data.

4. **Computational Resources**:
   - **Traditional Machine Learning**: Generally requires less computational power and can run on standard hardware.
   - **Deep Learning**: Demands significant computational resources, often necessitating the use of GPUs or TPUs for training and

inference.

5. **Performance**:

  - **Traditional Machine Learning**: May perform well on simple tasks but may struggle with tasks involving complex patterns and high-dimensional data.

  - **Deep Learning**: Achieves state-of-the-art performance on complex tasks such as image and speech recognition, natural language processing, and game playing.

Conclusion

Deep learning has revolutionized the field of artificial intelligence by enabling the development of models that can learn complex patterns and representations from large amounts of data. In this chapter, we explored the importance of deep learning, the role of big data and computing power, common deep learning frameworks, and key differences between deep learning and traditional machine learning.

By understanding these fundamentals, you can appreciate the power and potential of deep learning in various AI applications. As we continue our journey through the subsequent chapters, we will delve deeper into specific deep learning architectures and their practical applications.

In the next chapter, we will explore Convolutional Neural Networks (CNNs), a type of deep learning architecture widely used for image recognition and computer vision tasks. We will examine how CNNs work, their key components, and practical use cases.

CHAPTER 13: CONVOLUTIONAL NEURAL NETWORKS (CNNS)

Overview

Convolutional Neural Networks (CNNs) are a specialized type of deep learning architecture designed for processing structured grid data, such as images. CNNs have revolutionized the field of computer vision, enabling significant advancements in tasks like image recognition, object detection, and image segmentation. In this chapter, we will delve into the workings of CNNs, their key components, and practical use cases. By understanding these concepts, you will gain insight into how CNNs have become the backbone of many modern computer vision applications.

Architecture of Convolutional Neural Networks

Definition: A Convolutional Neural Network (CNN) is a deep learning model that uses convolutional layers to extract features from input data. The architecture of a CNN is composed of multiple layers, each serving a specific purpose in the feature extraction and classification process.

Key Components of CNNs:

1. **Convolutional Layers:**
   - **Function:** Convolutional layers apply a set of

learnable filters (kernels) to the input data to extract features such as edges, textures, and patterns.

- **Operation:** The filter slides over the input data, performing element-wise multiplication and summing the results to produce a feature map (also known as an activation map).
- **Stride:** The step size by which the filter moves across the input data. A larger stride reduces the spatial dimensions of the output feature map.
- **Padding:** Adding extra pixels around the input data to control the spatial dimensions of the output feature map. Common padding methods include "valid" (no padding) and "same" (padding to keep the output size equal to the input size).

2. **Pooling Layers:**

- **Function:** Pooling layers reduce the spatial dimensions of the feature maps, reducing the number of parameters and computational complexity while retaining important features.
- **Types:** The most common pooling methods are max pooling and average pooling. Max pooling selects the maximum value from a patch of the feature map, while average pooling calculates the average value.
- **Operation:** The pooling layer slides a window over the feature map, applying the pooling function to each patch and producing a downsampled output.

3. **Fully Connected Layers:**

- **Function:** Fully connected layers, also known

as dense layers, connect every neuron in the layer to every neuron in the previous layer. They are used to integrate the features extracted by the convolutional and pooling layers and produce the final output.

- **Operation:** The output from the previous layer is flattened into a one-dimensional vector and passed through the fully connected layers for classification or regression.

4. **Activation Functions:**

- **Function:** Activation functions introduce non-linearity into the network, enabling it to learn complex patterns.

- **Common Activation Functions:** ReLU (Rectified Linear Unit), sigmoid, tanh, and softmax (for multi-class classification).

5. **Dropout Layers:**

- **Function:** Dropout layers randomly set a fraction of the input neurons to zero during training to prevent overfitting and improve generalization.

- **Operation:** A dropout rate is specified, which determines the fraction of neurons to drop.

How CNNs Work

Forward Propagation:

1. **Input Layer:**

- The input layer receives the raw image data, typically represented as a multi-dimensional array (e.g., height x width x channels for RGB images).

2. **Convolutional Layers:**

- Convolutional layers apply filters to the input

data to produce feature maps that capture local patterns and features.

3. **Pooling Layers:**
   - Pooling layers downsample the feature maps, reducing their spatial dimensions while retaining important information.

4. **Additional Convolutional and Pooling Layers:**
   - A CNN may have multiple convolutional and pooling layers to progressively extract higher-level features from the input data.

5. **Fully Connected Layers:**
   - The flattened output from the final pooling layer is passed through fully connected layers to produce the final output (e.g., class probabilities).

6. **Output Layer:**
   - The output layer produces the final prediction, such as the class label for an image.

Backward Propagation (Backpropagation):

1. **Loss Calculation:**
   - The loss function calculates the difference between the predicted output and the actual target. Common loss functions for CNNs include cross-entropy loss for classification tasks and mean squared error for regression tasks.

2. **Gradient Computation:**
   - The gradients of the loss function with respect to the network's weights and biases are computed using the chain rule of calculus.

3. **Weight and Bias Updates:**
   - The weights and biases are updated using

an optimization algorithm, such as stochastic gradient descent (SGD) or Adam, to minimize the loss function.

4. **Iteration:**

   ◦ The forward and backward propagation steps are repeated for multiple epochs until the network converges to an optimal solution.

Applications of Convolutional Neural Networks

1. **Image Classification:**

   ◦ **Description:** Image classification involves assigning a label to an input image from a predefined set of categories.

   ◦ **Use Case:** Classifying images of animals (e.g., cat, dog, bird), handwritten digit recognition (e.g., MNIST dataset).

2. **Object Detection:**

   ◦ **Description:** Object detection involves identifying and localizing objects within an image by drawing bounding boxes around them.

   ◦ **Use Case:** Detecting and labeling objects in real-time video feeds, such as pedestrians, vehicles, and traffic signs.

3. **Image Segmentation:**

   ◦ **Description:** Image segmentation involves partitioning an image into multiple segments or regions, each corresponding to a specific object or area.

   ◦ **Use Case:** Medical image analysis (e.g., segmenting tumors in MRI scans), autonomous driving (e.g., road and lane detection).

4. **Face Recognition:**

- **Description:** Face recognition involves identifying or verifying individuals based on facial features.
- **Use Case:** Security and surveillance systems, authentication for mobile devices.

5. **Image Generation:**

- **Description:** Image generation involves creating new images based on learned patterns from a dataset.
- **Use Case:** Generating realistic images using generative adversarial networks (GANs), style transfer (e.g., converting photos to artistic styles).

Practical Example: Building a Simple CNN for Image Classification

Dataset:

- We will use the CIFAR-10 dataset, which consists of 60,000 32x32 color images in 10 classes (e.g., airplanes, cars, birds, cats).

Steps:

1. **Data Preparation:**

- Load and preprocess the CIFAR-10 dataset (e.g., normalization, data augmentation).

2. **Model Architecture:**

- Define the CNN architecture, including convolutional layers, pooling layers, and fully connected layers.

3. **Compilation:**

- Compile the model with an appropriate optimizer (e.g., Adam) and loss function (e.g., categorical cross-entropy).

4. **Training:**

- Train the model on the training data using a validation set to monitor performance and prevent overfitting.

5. **Evaluation:**

   - Evaluate the model on the test data using accuracy and other relevant metrics.

6. **Prediction:**

   - Use the trained model to make predictions on new, unseen images.

Sample Code (using TensorFlow/Keras):

python

```
import tensorflow as tf
from tensorflow.keras import layers, models
from tensorflow.keras.datasets import cifar10

# Load and preprocess the CIFAR-10 dataset
(train_images, train_labels), (test_images, test_labels) = cifar10.load_data()
train_images, test_images = train_images / 255.0, test_images / 255.0

# Define the CNN architecture
model = models.Sequential([
    layers.Conv2D(32, (3, 3), activation='relu', input_shape=(32, 32, 3)),
    layers.MaxPooling2D((2, 2)),
    layers.Conv2D(64, (3, 3), activation='relu'),
    layers.MaxPooling2D((2, 2)),
    layers.Conv2D(64, (3, 3), activation='relu'),
    layers.Flatten(),
    layers.Dense(64, activation='relu'),
    layers.Dense(10, activation='softmax')
])

# Compile the model
model.compile(optimizer='adam',
          loss='sparse_categorical_crossentropy',
          metrics=['accuracy'])

# Train the model
model.fit(train_images,             train_labels,              epochs=10,
validation_data=(test_images, test_labels))

# Evaluate the model
test_loss, test_acc = model.evaluate(test_images, test_labels, verbose=2)
```

```
print(f'Test accuracy: {test_acc}')
```

```
# Make predictions
predictions = model.predict(test_images)
```

Conclusion

Convolutional Neural Networks (CNNs) are a powerful and versatile deep learning architecture that has revolutionized the field of computer vision. In this chapter, we explored the architecture of CNNs, including key components such as convolutional layers, pooling layers, and fully connected layers. We also discussed how CNNs work, including forward and backward propagation, and examined various applications of CNNs in image classification, object detection, image segmentation, face recognition, and image generation.

By understanding the principles and applications of CNNs, you can leverage their capabilities to solve complex computer vision tasks and develop state-of-the-art models. As we continue our journey through the subsequent chapters, we will delve deeper into more advanced neural network architectures and their practical applications.

In the next chapter, we will explore Recurrent Neural Networks (RNNs), a type of deep learning architecture designed for sequence data and tasks such as language modeling and time series prediction. We will examine how R

CHAPTER 14: RECURRENT NEURAL NETWORKS (RNNS)

Overview

Recurrent Neural Networks (RNNs) are a specialized type of deep learning architecture designed for processing sequential data. They excel at tasks where the order of the input data is crucial, such as time series prediction, language modeling, and natural language processing. In this chapter, we will explore the workings of RNNs, their key components, the challenges associated with training RNNs, and practical use cases. By understanding these concepts, you will gain insights into how RNNs handle sequential data and their applications in various domains.

Architecture of Recurrent Neural Networks

Definition: A Recurrent Neural Network (RNN) is a type of neural network that introduces loops in its architecture, allowing information to persist across time steps. This design makes RNNs well-suited for tasks involving sequential data, where past information is relevant to the current prediction.

Key Components of RNNs:

1. **Recurrent Cells:**
   - **Function:** Recurrent cells are the building blocks of RNNs. They process input data at each time step and maintain an internal

hidden state that captures information from previous time steps.

- **Operation:** At each time step tt, the recurrent cell receives the current input xtx_t and the previous hidden state ht−1h_{t-1}. It updates the hidden state hth_t based on these inputs.

2. **Hidden State:**

- **Function:** The hidden state is an internal memory that stores information about the sequence. It is updated at each time step and used to influence future predictions.
- **Operation:** The hidden state hth_t is calculated using the current input xtx_t, the previous hidden state ht−1h_{t-1}, and learnable parameters (weights and biases).

3. **Output Layer:**

- **Function:** The output layer generates the final predictions based on the hidden state. The type of output depends on the specific task (e.g., classification, regression).
- **Operation:** The output yty_t at each time step is calculated using the hidden state hth_t and a set of learnable parameters.

Equations:

- Hidden state update: ht=σ(Wh·xt+Uh·ht−1+bh)h_t = $\sigma(W_h \cdot x_t + U_h \cdot h_{t-1} + b_h)$
- Output calculation: yt=φ(Wy·ht+by)y_t = $\phi(W_y \cdot h_t + b_y)$
- Where Wh,Uh,W_h, U_h, and WyW_y are weight matrices, bhb_h and byb_y are biases, σ\sigma is the activation function (e.g., tanh or ReLU), and φ\phi is the output activation function (e.g., softmax for classification).

Types of RNNs

1. **Vanilla RNN:**
   - **Description:** The basic form of RNN that uses standard recurrent cells. While effective for certain tasks, vanilla RNNs are prone to issues such as vanishing and exploding gradients.
   - **Use Cases:** Simple sequence prediction tasks, toy problems.

2. **Long Short-Term Memory (LSTM):**
   - **Description:** LSTM is an advanced type of RNN designed to address the vanishing gradient problem. It introduces memory cells and gates (input, output, forget) to control the flow of information.
   - **Components:**
     - **Memory Cell:** Stores information over long time periods.
     - **Input Gate:** Controls the update of the memory cell with new input.
     - **Forget Gate:** Controls the removal of irrelevant information from the memory cell.
     - **Output Gate:** Controls the output of the memory cell to the hidden state.
   - **Use Cases:** Language modeling, speech recognition, time series prediction, text generation.

3. **Gated Recurrent Unit (GRU):**
   - **Description:** GRU is a simplified variant of LSTM that combines the input and forget gates into a single update gate and uses a reset gate. It retains the ability to handle long-term dependencies while being computationally

efficient.

- ○ **Components:**
  - ▪ **Update Gate:** Controls the update of the hidden state.
  - ▪ **Reset Gate:** Controls the reset of the hidden state.
- ○ **Use Cases:** Similar to LSTM, used in language modeling, speech recognition, and time series prediction.

4. **Bidirectional RNN (Bi-RNN):**

- ○ **Description:** Bi-RNN consists of two RNNs, one processing the sequence forward and the other processing it backward. This allows the model to capture information from both past and future time steps.
- ○ **Use Cases:** Machine translation, named entity recognition, sentiment analysis.

Challenges in Training RNNs

1. **Vanishing Gradient Problem:**

- ○ **Description:** During backpropagation, gradients can become very small, making it difficult for the model to learn long-term dependencies.
- ○ **Solution:** Use advanced RNN variants like LSTM and GRU that are designed to mitigate the vanishing gradient problem.

2. **Exploding Gradient Problem:**

- ○ **Description:** During backpropagation, gradients can become very large, causing instability in the learning process.
- ○ **Solution:** Apply gradient clipping, a technique that limits the magnitude of gradients to prevent them from exploding.

3. **Computational Complexity:**
   - **Description:** Training RNNs can be computationally intensive, especially for long sequences.
   - **Solution:** Use parallelization techniques, efficient hardware (GPUs or TPUs), and optimized frameworks to accelerate training.

4. **Sequence Length:**
   - **Description:** RNNs can struggle with very long sequences, as maintaining information over many time steps is challenging.
   - **Solution:** Use hierarchical RNNs, attention mechanisms, or transformers to handle long sequences effectively.

Applications of Recurrent Neural Networks

1. **Language Modeling:**
   - **Description:** Language modeling involves predicting the next word or character in a sequence based on the previous context.
   - **Use Case:** Text generation, autocomplete, machine translation.

2. **Time Series Prediction:**
   - **Description:** Time series prediction involves forecasting future values based on historical data.
   - **Use Case:** Stock price prediction, weather forecasting, demand forecasting.

3. **Speech Recognition:**
   - **Description:** Speech recognition involves converting spoken language into text.
   - **Use Case:** Voice assistants (e.g., Siri, Alexa), transcription services, real-time translation.

4. **Text Generation:**

  ◦ **Description:** Text generation involves creating coherent and contextually relevant text based on a given prompt.
  ◦ **Use Case:** Creative writing, chatbots, automated content creation.

5. **Sentiment Analysis:**

  ◦ **Description:** Sentiment analysis involves determining the sentiment or emotion expressed in a piece of text.
  ◦ **Use Case:** Social media monitoring, customer feedback analysis, opinion mining.

6. **Machine Translation:**

  ◦ **Description:** Machine translation involves translating text from one language to another.
  ◦ **Use Case:** Translation services (e.g., Google Translate), multilingual communication, localization.

Practical Example: Building a Simple RNN for Language Modeling

Dataset:

  • We will use a dataset of text sequences, such as the text from a book or collection of articles.

Steps:

1. **Data Preparation:**

  ◦ Load and preprocess the text data (e.g., tokenization, encoding, sequence generation).

2. **Model Architecture:**

  ◦ Define the RNN architecture, including recurrent layers (e.g., LSTM, GRU) and fully connected layers.

3. **Compilation:**

   ◦ Compile the model with an appropriate optimizer (e.g., Adam) and loss function (e.g., categorical cross-entropy).

4. **Training:**

   ◦ Train the model on the text sequences using a validation set to monitor performance and prevent overfitting.

5. **Evaluation:**

   ◦ Evaluate the model on the test data using relevant metrics (e.g., perplexity, accuracy).

6. **Prediction:**

   ◦ Use the trained model to generate text based on a given prompt.

Sample Code (using TensorFlow/Keras):

python

```python
import tensorflow as tf
from tensorflow.keras import layers, models
from tensorflow.keras.preprocessing.text import Tokenizer
from tensorflow.keras.preprocessing.sequence import pad_sequences
import numpy as np

# Sample text data
text = "In the beginning God created the heaven and the earth. And the earth was without form, and void; and darkness was upon the face of the deep..."

# Tokenize and encode the text
tokenizer = Tokenizer()
tokenizer.fit_on_texts([text])
encoded_text = tokenizer.texts_to_sequences([text])[0]

# Generate input-output pairs for training
sequence_length = 5
sequences = []
for i in range(sequence_length, len(encoded_text)):
    sequence = encoded_text[i-sequence_length:i+1]
    sequences.append(sequence)
sequences = np.array(sequences)
```

```
# Split into input (X) and output (y)
X, y = sequences[:, :-1], sequences[:, -1]
y = tf.keras.utils.to_categorical(y, num_classes=len(tokenizer.word_index) +
1)

# Define the RNN architecture
model = models.Sequential([
    layers.Embedding(input_dim=len(tokenizer.word_index)        +        1,
output_dim=10, input_length=sequence_length),
    layers.LSTM(50, return_sequences=False),
    layers.Dense(len(tokenizer.word_index) + 1, activation='softmax')
])

# Compile the model
model.compile(optimizer='adam',              loss='categorical_crossentropy',
metrics=['accuracy'])

# Train the model
model
```

CHAPTER 15: GENERATIVE ADVERSARIAL NETWORKS (GANS)

Overview

Generative Adversarial Networks (GANs) are a revolutionary type of deep learning architecture that have gained significant attention for their ability to generate realistic synthetic data, such as images, videos, and audio. GANs consist of two neural networks, a generator and a discriminator, that work together in a competitive setting to improve the quality of generated data. In this chapter, we will explore the architecture of GANs, how they work, key components, challenges, and practical applications. By understanding these concepts, you will gain insights into how GANs have transformed various fields, including computer vision, art, and data augmentation.

Architecture of Generative Adversarial Networks

Definition: Generative Adversarial Networks (GANs) consist of two neural networks, the generator and the discriminator, that are trained simultaneously in a process known as adversarial training. The generator aims to create realistic synthetic data, while the discriminator attempts to distinguish between real and synthetic data.

Key Components of GANs:

1. **Generator:**
   - **Function:** The generator is responsible for producing synthetic data from random noise. It learns to create data that resembles the real data distribution.
   - **Operation:** The generator takes a random noise vector (usually sampled from a Gaussian distribution) as input and transforms it through multiple layers to produce synthetic data.

2. **Discriminator:**
   - **Function:** The discriminator is responsible for distinguishing between real and synthetic data. It learns to differentiate between authentic data samples and those generated by the generator.
   - **Operation:** The discriminator receives either real data or synthetic data as input and outputs a probability score indicating whether the input data is real or fake.

Adversarial Training:
   - **Objective:** The generator and discriminator are trained simultaneously in a competitive setting. The generator's objective is to create data that can fool the discriminator, while the discriminator's objective is to accurately classify real and synthetic data.
   - **Loss Functions:** The generator and discriminator have separate loss functions:
      - **Generator's Loss:** Measures the ability of the generator to fool the discriminator. Typically, the generator's loss is the negative log probability of the discriminator being fooled.
      - **Discriminator's Loss:** Measures the accuracy

of the discriminator in distinguishing real from synthetic data. The discriminator's loss is the sum of the negative log probabilities of correctly classifying real and synthetic data.

Equations:

- Generator's loss: $\mathcal{L}_G = -\log(D(G(z)))$

- Discriminator's loss: $\mathcal{L}_D = -\left[\log(D(x)) + \log(1 - D(G(z)))\right]$

- Where $D(x)$ is the discriminator's probability that real data x is real, $D(G(z))$ is the discriminator's probability that synthetic data $G(z)$ is real, and z is the random noise vector.

How GANs Work

Training Process:

1. **Initialization:**
   - Initialize the generator and discriminator with random weights and biases.

2. **Forward Pass (Discriminator):**
   - Feed a batch of real data and a batch of synthetic data (generated by the generator) into the discriminator.
   - Calculate the discriminator's loss based on its ability to classify real and synthetic data correctly.

3. **Backward Pass (Discriminator):**
   - Update the discriminator's weights and biases using the gradients of the discriminator's loss with respect to its parameters.

4. **Forward Pass (Generator):**
   - Generate a batch of synthetic data using the generator.

- Feed the synthetic data into the discriminator to obtain the probability scores.
- Calculate the generator's loss based on its ability to fool the discriminator.

5. **Backward Pass (Generator):**
   - Update the generator's weights and biases using the gradients of the generator's loss with respect to its parameters.

6. **Iteration:**
   - Repeat the forward and backward passes for both the generator and discriminator for multiple iterations (epochs) until the generated data is indistinguishable from the real data.

Challenges in Training GANs

1. **Mode Collapse:**
   - **Description:** The generator produces a limited variety of outputs, resulting in a lack of diversity in the generated data.
   - **Solution:** Use techniques such as mini-batch discrimination, feature matching, and unrolled GANs to encourage diversity in the generated data.

2. **Training Instability:**
   - **Description:** The training process of GANs can be unstable, with the generator and discriminator oscillating or diverging.
   - **Solution:** Use techniques such as spectral normalization, Wasserstein GAN (WGAN), and gradient penalty to stabilize the training process.

3. **Evaluation Metrics:**
   - **Description:** Evaluating the quality of

generated data can be challenging, as traditional metrics may not fully capture the realism and diversity of the data.

- **Solution:** Use metrics such as Inception Score (IS), Frechet Inception Distance (FID), and human evaluation to assess the quality of the generated data.

4. **Computational Complexity:**

- **Description:** Training GANs can be computationally intensive, requiring significant processing power and memory.

- **Solution:** Use efficient hardware (GPUs or TPUs), optimized frameworks, and techniques such as progressive growing of GANs to reduce computational complexity.

Applications of Generative Adversarial Networks

1. **Image Generation:**

- **Description:** GANs are used to generate realistic images from random noise or other input data.

- **Use Case:** Creating high-resolution images, generating synthetic faces, style transfer.

2. **Image-to-Image Translation:**

- **Description:** GANs can translate images from one domain to another while preserving the content.

- **Use Case:** Converting sketches to realistic images, translating night images to day images, generating photorealistic images from segmentation maps.

3. **Text-to-Image Synthesis:**

- **Description:** GANs can generate images from textual descriptions, enabling the creation of visuals based on textual input.

- ○ **Use Case:** Generating images of birds, flowers, or objects based on descriptive text.

4. **Data Augmentation:**

- ○ **Description:** GANs can generate additional training data to augment existing datasets, improving the performance of machine learning models.
- ○ **Use Case:** Generating synthetic data for medical imaging, enhancing datasets for object detection, creating diverse training samples for facial recognition.

5. **Video Generation:**

- ○ **Description:** GANs can generate realistic video sequences from random noise or input frames.
- ○ **Use Case:** Creating animated videos, generating video frames for autonomous driving simulations.

6. **Anomaly Detection:**

- ○ **Description:** GANs can be used to detect anomalies by learning the distribution of normal data and identifying deviations.
- ○ **Use Case:** Detecting fraudulent transactions, identifying defects in manufacturing, monitoring network security.

7. **Creative Art and Design:**

- ○ **Description:** GANs enable artists and designers to create unique and novel artworks by generating visuals based on learned patterns.
- ○ **Use Case:** Creating digital art, designing fashion items, generating music.

Practical Example: Building a Simple GAN for Image Generation

Dataset:

- We will use the MNIST dataset, which consists of 28x28 grayscale images of handwritten digits.

Steps:

1. **Data Preparation:**
   - Load and preprocess the MNIST dataset (e.g., normalization).

2. **Model Architecture:**
   - Define the generator and discriminator architectures using convolutional layers and activation functions.

3. **Compilation:**
   - Compile the generator and discriminator with appropriate optimizers (e.g., Adam) and loss functions (e.g., binary cross-entropy).

4. **Training:**
   - Train the GAN using the adversarial training process, updating the generator and discriminator iteratively.

5. **Evaluation:**
   - Evaluate the quality of the generated images using relevant metrics and visual inspection.

Sample Code (using TensorFlow/Keras):

```python
python
import tensorflow as tf
from tensorflow.keras import layers, models
from tensorflow.keras.datasets import mnist
import numpy as np
import matplotlib.pyplot as plt

# Load and preprocess the MNIST dataset
(train_images, _), (_, _) = mnist.load_data()
```

```python
train_images    =    train_images.reshape(train_images.shape[0],    28,    28,
1).astype('float32')
train_images = (train_images - 127.5) / 127.5  # Normalize to [-1, 1]

# Define the generator architecture
def build_generator():
    model = models.Sequential([
        layers.Dense(256, input_shape=(100,), activation='relu'),
        layers.BatchNormalization(),
        layers.Dense(512, activation='relu'),
        layers.BatchNormalization(),
        layers.Dense(1024, activation='relu'),
        layers.BatchNormalization(),
        layers.Dense(28*28*1, activation='tanh'),
        layers.Reshape((28, 28, 1))
    ])
    return model

# Define the discriminator architecture
def build_discriminator():
    model = models.Sequential([
        layers.Flatten(input_shape=(28, 28, 1)),
        layers.Dense(512, activation='relu'),
        layers.Dense(256, activation='relu'),
        layers.Dense(1, activation='sigmoid')
    ])
    return model

# Build and compile the generator and discriminator
generator = build_generator()
discriminator = build_discriminator()
discriminator.compile(optimizer='adam',          loss='binary_crossentropy',
metrics=['accuracy'])

# Define the GAN model (generator + discriminator)
discriminator.trainable = False
gan_input = layers.Input(shape=(100,))
generated_image = generator(gan_input)
gan_output = discriminator(generated
```

CHAPTER 16: NATURAL LANGUAGE PROCESSING (NLP)

Overview

Natural Language Processing (NLP) is a subfield of artificial intelligence that focuses on the interaction between computers and human language. NLP enables machines to understand, interpret, and generate human language, making it possible for computers to perform tasks such as language translation, sentiment analysis, and text generation. In this chapter, we will explore the key tasks and techniques in NLP, including tokenization, named entity recognition, sentiment analysis, and transformer models like BERT. By understanding these concepts, you will gain insights into how NLP powers many modern applications and services.

Key Tasks in NLP

1. **Tokenization:**

   - **Definition:** Tokenization is the process of breaking down text into smaller units called tokens, which can be words, phrases, or characters. Tokens are the basic building blocks for many NLP tasks.

   - **Types:**

     - **Word Tokenization:** Splitting text into individual words (e.g., "Natural language processing" becomes ["Natural", "language", "processing"]).

- **Sentence Tokenization:** Splitting text into sentences (e.g., "I love NLP. It is fascinating." becomes ["I love NLP.", "It is fascinating."]).

  ○ **Applications:** Preprocessing step for text analysis, indexing for search engines, language modeling.

2. **Named Entity Recognition (NER):**

   ○ **Definition:** Named Entity Recognition (NER) is the process of identifying and classifying named entities in text into predefined categories such as person names, organizations, locations, dates, and more.

   ○ **Example:** "Barack Obama was the 44th President of the United States" -> [("Barack Obama", "PERSON"), ("United States", "LOCATION")].

   ○ **Applications:** Information extraction, content classification, question answering systems.

3. **Sentiment Analysis:**

   ○ **Definition:** Sentiment analysis is the process of determining the sentiment or emotion expressed in a piece of text. It can classify text as positive, negative, neutral, or identify specific emotions like joy, anger, or sadness.

   ○ **Example:** "I am so happy with the service" -> Positive sentiment.

   ○ **Applications:** Social media monitoring, customer feedback analysis, brand reputation management.

4. **Part-of-Speech Tagging (POS Tagging):**
  - **Definition:** Part-of-Speech (POS) tagging is the process of assigning grammatical categories (e.g., noun, verb, adjective) to each word in a sentence.
  - **Example:** "The quick brown fox jumps over the lazy dog" -> [("The", "DET"), ("quick", "ADJ"), ("brown", "ADJ"), ("fox", "NOUN"), ("jumps", "VERB"), ("over", "ADP"), ("the", "DET"), ("lazy", "ADJ"), ("dog", "NOUN")].
  - **Applications:** Syntax parsing, language modeling, text-to-speech systems.

5. **Machine Translation:**
  - **Definition:** Machine translation is the process of automatically translating text from one language to another.
  - **Example:** Translating "Hello, how are you?" from English to Spanish -> "Hola, ¿cómo estás?".
  - **Applications:** Translation services (e.g., Google Translate), multilingual communication, localization.

6. **Text Generation:**
  - **Definition:** Text generation involves creating coherent and contextually relevant text based on a given input or prompt.
  - **Example:** Given the prompt "Once upon a time," the model generates a complete story.
  - **Applications:** Creative writing, chatbots, automated content creation.

Key Techniques in NLP

1. **Bag of Words (BoW):**
  - **Definition:** Bag of Words is a simple

representation of text that treats each document as an unordered collection of words. It creates a vocabulary of known words and uses word frequency to represent each document.

- **Limitations:** Ignores word order and context, leading to a loss of semantic meaning.

2. **TF-IDF (Term Frequency-Inverse Document Frequency):**

- **Definition:** TF-IDF is a statistical measure that evaluates the importance of a word in a document relative to a collection of documents (corpus). It is calculated as the product of term frequency (TF) and inverse document frequency (IDF).

- **Limitations:** Still treats text as a bag of words, ignoring word order and context.

3. **Word Embeddings:**

- **Definition:** Word embeddings are dense vector representations of words that capture semantic meaning and relationships between words. Common methods for generating word embeddings include Word2Vec, GloVe, and FastText.

- **Advantages:** Capture semantic meaning and relationships between words, useful for various NLP tasks.

4. **Recurrent Neural Networks (RNNs) and LSTMs:**

- **Definition:** RNNs and Long Short-Term Memory (LSTM) networks are designed to handle sequential data and capture dependencies between words in a sequence. They are commonly used for tasks such as language modeling and text generation.

- ◦ **Limitations:** May struggle with long-term dependencies and require significant computational resources.

5. **Attention Mechanisms:**

   - ◦ **Definition:** Attention mechanisms allow models to focus on specific parts of the input sequence when making predictions, improving the ability to capture long-term dependencies.
   - ◦ **Applications:** Machine translation, text summarization, question answering.

6. **Transformer Models:**

   - ◦ **Definition:** Transformer models are a type of neural network architecture that relies entirely on self-attention mechanisms to process input data. Transformers have become the state-of-the-art approach for many NLP tasks.
   - ◦ **Examples:** BERT (Bidirectional Encoder Representations from Transformers), GPT-3 (Generative Pre-trained Transformer 3), T5 (Text-To-Text Transfer Transformer).
   - ◦ **Advantages:** Handle long-range dependencies effectively, parallelizable for faster training.

Transformer Models: BERT and GPT-3

1. **BERT (Bidirectional Encoder Representations from Transformers):**

   - ◦ **Description:** BERT is a pre-trained transformer model designed to understand the context of words in a sentence bidirectionally. It uses masked language modeling and next sentence prediction for pre-training.

- Key Features:
  - **Masked Language Modeling:** Randomly masks some tokens in the input and trains the model to predict them.
  - **Next Sentence Prediction:** Trains the model to predict whether two given sentences follow each other in the text.
- **Applications:** Question answering, text classification, named entity recognition.

2. **GPT-3 (Generative Pre-trained Transformer 3):**

- **Description:** GPT-3 is a generative transformer model that excels at text generation and completion tasks. It is pre-trained on a large corpus of text data and fine-tuned for specific tasks.
- Key Features:
  - **Unidirectional Training:** GPT-3 generates text by predicting the next word in a sequence based on the context of previous words.
  - **Zero-shot, One-shot, and Few-shot Learning:** GPT-3 can perform tasks with little to no task-specific training data.
- **Applications:** Text generation, language translation, conversational agents, creative writing.

Applications of NLP

1. **Virtual Assistants:**

- **Description:** NLP powers virtual assistants like Siri, Alexa, and Google Assistant, enabling them to understand and respond to user queries.

- **Use Case:** Voice-activated commands, information retrieval, task automation.

2. **Sentiment Analysis:**
   - **Description:** NLP techniques are used to analyze social media posts, reviews, and feedback to determine public sentiment and opinion.
   - **Use Case:** Brand monitoring, customer feedback analysis, market research.

3. **Machine Translation:**
   - **Description:** NLP models are used to translate text from one language to another, facilitating multilingual communication.
   - **Use Case:** Translation services, localization of content, international communication.

4. **Text Summarization:**
   - **Description:** NLP techniques are used to generate concise summaries of long documents, making it easier to extract key information.
   - **Use Case:** News summarization, document summarization, content aggregation.

5. **Information Retrieval:**
   - **Description:** NLP is used to develop search engines and information retrieval systems that can understand and retrieve relevant documents based on user queries.
   - **Use Case:** Search engines, digital libraries, knowledge bases.

6. **Chatbots and Conversational Agents:**
   - **Description:** NLP powers chatbots and

conversational agents that can engage in natural language conversations with users.

- **Use Case:** Customer support, virtual assistants, interactive applications.

Practical Example: Building a Simple NLP Model for Sentiment Analysis

Dataset:

- We will use the IMDb movie reviews dataset, which contains labeled reviews as positive or negative.

Steps:

1. **Data Preparation:**
   - Load and preprocess the IMDb dataset (e.g., tokenization, encoding, padding).

2. **Model Architecture:**
   - Define a neural network architecture for sentiment analysis using embedding layers, LSTM layers, and dense layers.

3. **Compilation:**
   - Compile the model with an appropriate optimizer (e.g., Adam) and loss function (e.g., binary cross-entropy).

4. **Training:**
   - Train the model on the training data using a validation set to monitor performance and prevent overfitting.

5. **Evaluation:**
   - Evaluate the model on the test data using accuracy and other relevant metrics.

6. **Prediction:**
   - Use the trained model to predict the sentiment of new, unseen reviews.

Sample Code (using TensorFlow/Keras):

python

```
import tensorflow as tf
from tensorflow.keras import layers, models
from tensorflow.keras.datasets import imdb
from tensorflow
```

CHAPTER 17:
COMPUTER VISION

Overview

Computer Vision is a field of artificial intelligence that enables machines to interpret and understand visual information from the world. It involves processing and analyzing images and videos to extract meaningful insights and perform tasks such as object detection, image classification, and image segmentation. In this chapter, we will explore the fundamentals of computer vision, key techniques and algorithms, practical applications, and the challenges associated with developing computer vision systems.

Fundamentals of Computer Vision

Definition: Computer vision involves the development of algorithms and models that can process visual data (images and videos) to perform tasks that typically require human vision.

Key Concepts:

1. **Pixels:** The smallest unit of an image, representing a single point of color. Images are composed of a grid of pixels.

2. **Color Spaces:** Different ways to represent color in images, such as RGB (Red, Green, Blue), grayscale, HSV (Hue, Saturation, Value), and others.

3. **Resolution:** The number of pixels in an image, typically described in terms of width x height. Higher resolution means more detail.

Key Techniques and Algorithms in Computer Vision

1. **Image Classification:**
   - **Definition:** The task of assigning a label to an entire image based on its content. Image classification models are trained to recognize patterns and features that correspond to specific categories.
   - **Example:** Classifying images of animals into categories such as cats, dogs, and birds.
   - **Algorithms:** Convolutional Neural Networks (CNNs) are widely used for image classification tasks due to their ability to capture spatial hierarchies in images.

2. **Object Detection:**
   - **Definition:** The task of identifying and localizing objects within an image by drawing bounding boxes around them. Object detection models not only classify objects but also determine their positions.
   - **Example:** Detecting and labeling objects such as cars, pedestrians, and traffic signs in street images.
   - **Algorithms:** Region-based CNNs (R-CNN), YOLO (You Only Look Once), and SSD (Single Shot MultiBox Detector) are popular object detection algorithms.

3. **Image Segmentation:**
   - **Definition:** The task of partitioning an image into multiple segments or regions, each corresponding to a specific object or area. Image segmentation provides pixel-level information about the objects in an image.
   - **Example:** Segmenting medical images to

identify and isolate tumors.

- **Algorithms:** Fully Convolutional Networks (FCNs), U-Net, and Mask R-CNN are commonly used for image segmentation tasks.

4. **Facial Recognition:**

- **Definition:** The task of identifying or verifying individuals based on their facial features. Facial recognition models analyze facial landmarks and patterns to match faces against a database of known individuals.
- **Example:** Unlocking a smartphone using facial recognition technology.
- **Algorithms:** DeepFace, FaceNet, and MTCNN (Multi-task Cascaded Convolutional Networks) are well-known facial recognition models.

5. **Optical Character Recognition (OCR):**

- **Definition:** The task of extracting text from images or scanned documents. OCR systems convert visual representations of text into machine-readable text.
- **Example:** Digitizing printed documents, extracting text from license plates.
- **Algorithms:** Tesseract OCR, EAST (Efficient and Accurate Scene Text Detector), and CRNN (Convolutional Recurrent Neural Network) are popular OCR algorithms.

6. **Image Generation:**

- **Definition:** The task of generating new images based on learned patterns from a dataset. Image generation models can create realistic visuals from random noise or other input data.

- **Example:** Generating photorealistic images of human faces using GANs (Generative Adversarial Networks).
- **Algorithms:** GANs, Variational Autoencoders (VAEs), and StyleGAN are widely used for image generation tasks.

Applications of Computer Vision

1. **Autonomous Vehicles:**
   - **Description:** Computer vision is essential for autonomous vehicles to perceive and navigate the environment. Vision systems enable vehicles to detect and recognize objects, lane markings, and traffic signs.
   - **Use Case:** Self-driving cars, autonomous drones, delivery robots.

2. **Medical Imaging:**
   - **Description:** Computer vision aids in the analysis and interpretation of medical images, facilitating early diagnosis and treatment planning.
   - **Use Case:** Detecting tumors in MRI scans, analyzing X-rays, segmenting organs in CT scans.

3. **Retail and E-commerce:**
   - **Description:** Computer vision enhances the shopping experience by enabling visual search, virtual try-ons, and inventory management.
   - **Use Case:** Visual search engines, virtual fitting rooms, automated checkout systems.

4. **Security and Surveillance:**
   - **Description:** Computer vision improves

security and surveillance systems by enabling real-time monitoring and anomaly detection.

- **Use Case:** Facial recognition for access control, detecting suspicious behavior, monitoring public spaces.

5. **Agriculture:**

- **Description:** Computer vision supports precision agriculture by monitoring crop health, detecting diseases, and optimizing resource use.
- **Use Case:** Crop monitoring, weed detection, yield estimation.

6. **Manufacturing and Industry:**

- **Description:** Computer vision enhances industrial automation by enabling quality control, defect detection, and predictive maintenance.
- **Use Case:** Inspecting products on production lines, detecting defects in manufacturing, monitoring equipment health.

7. **Augmented Reality (AR) and Virtual Reality (VR):**

- **Description:** Computer vision powers AR and VR applications by enabling accurate tracking and rendering of virtual objects in real-world environments.
- **Use Case:** AR navigation, virtual training simulations, interactive gaming.

Challenges in Computer Vision

1. **Variability in Visual Data:**

- **Description:** Visual data can vary widely in terms of lighting, orientation, scale, and occlusion. Developing models that can generalize across different conditions is challenging.

- **Solution:** Use data augmentation techniques to introduce variability during training and improve model robustness.

2. **Annotation and Labeling:**

   - **Description:** Annotating and labeling large datasets for supervised learning is time-consuming and labor-intensive.
   - **Solution:** Use semi-supervised and unsupervised learning techniques, crowdsourcing, and synthetic data generation to reduce the reliance on labeled data.

3. **Computational Complexity:**

   - **Description:** Computer vision models, especially deep learning-based ones, are computationally intensive and require significant processing power and memory.
   - **Solution:** Use efficient hardware (GPUs or TPUs), optimized frameworks, and model compression techniques to reduce computational requirements.

4. **Real-time Processing:**

   - **Description:** Real-time applications, such as autonomous driving and surveillance, require fast and accurate processing of visual data.
   - **Solution:** Use lightweight models, efficient algorithms, and parallel processing to achieve real-time performance.

5. **Ethical and Privacy Concerns:**

   - **Description:** The widespread use of computer vision raises ethical and privacy concerns related to surveillance, facial recognition, and data security.

- **Solution:** Implement strict data privacy policies, ethical guidelines, and transparency measures to address these concerns.

Practical Example: Building a Simple Image Classification Model

Dataset:

- We will use the CIFAR-10 dataset, which consists of 60,000 32x32 color images in 10 classes (e.g., airplanes, cars, birds, cats).

Steps:

1. **Data Preparation:**
   - Load and preprocess the CIFAR-10 dataset (e.g., normalization, data augmentation).

2. **Model Architecture:**
   - Define a convolutional neural network (CNN) architecture for image classification, including convolutional layers, pooling layers, and fully connected layers.

3. **Compilation:**
   - Compile the model with an appropriate optimizer (e.g., Adam) and loss function (e.g., categorical cross-entropy).

4. **Training:**
   - Train the model on the training data using a validation set to monitor performance and prevent overfitting.

5. **Evaluation:**
   - Evaluate the model on the test data using accuracy and other relevant metrics.

6. **Prediction:**
   - Use the trained model to predict the classes of new, unseen images.

Sample Code (using TensorFlow/Keras):

python

```python
import tensorflow as tf
from tensorflow.keras import layers, models
from tensorflow.keras.datasets import cifar10

# Load and preprocess the CIFAR-10 dataset
(train_images, train_labels), (test_images, test_labels) = cifar10.load_data()
train_images, test_images = train_images / 255.0, test_images / 255.0

# Define the CNN architecture
model = models.Sequential([
    layers.Conv2D(32, (3, 3), activation='relu', input_shape=(32, 32, 3)),
    layers.MaxPooling2D((2, 2)),
    layers.Conv2D(64, (3, 3), activation='relu'),
    layers.MaxPooling2D((2, 2)),
    layers.Conv2D(64, (3, 3), activation='relu'),
    layers.Flatten(),
    layers.Dense(64, activation='relu'),
    layers.Dense(10, activation='softmax')
])

# Compile the model
model.compile(optimizer='adam',
          loss='sparse_categorical_crossentropy',
          metrics=['accuracy'])

# Train the model
model.fit(train_images,           train_labels,            epochs=10,
validation_data=(test_images, test_labels))

# Evaluate the model
test_loss, test_acc = model.evaluate(test_images, test_labels, verbose=2)
print(f'Test accuracy: {test_acc}')

# Make predictions
predictions = model.predict(test_images)
```

Conclusion

Computer vision is a dynamic field of artificial intelligence that enables

continue

Computer vision is a dynamic field of artificial intelligence that enables machines to interpret and understand visual information from the world. In this chapter, we explored the fundamentals of computer vision, key techniques and algorithms, practical applications, and the challenges associated with developing computer vision systems. We discussed various computer vision tasks, including image classification, object detection, image segmentation, facial recognition, OCR, and image generation.

By understanding these principles and applications, you can leverage computer vision technologies to solve complex visual tasks and develop innovative solutions in various domains. As we continue our journey through the subsequent chapters, we will delve deeper into more advanced AI topics and their practical applications.

In the next chapter, we will explore reinforcement learning, a type of machine learning that enables agents to learn by interacting with their environment and receiving feedback. We will examine the fundamentals of reinforcement learning, key concepts, algorithms, and practical use cases.

CHAPTER 18: REINFORCEMENT LEARNING

Overview

Reinforcement Learning (RL) is a type of machine learning where an agent learns to make decisions by interacting with its environment. The agent receives feedback in the form of rewards or penalties based on its actions and aims to maximize cumulative rewards over time. RL has gained significant attention for its success in solving complex problems, such as game playing, robotics, and autonomous systems. In this chapter, we will explore the fundamentals of reinforcement learning, key concepts, algorithms, and practical use cases. By understanding these principles, you will gain insights into how RL enables agents to learn and adapt in dynamic environments.

Fundamentals of Reinforcement Learning

Definition: Reinforcement learning involves training an agent to make a sequence of decisions by interacting with an environment. The agent's goal is to learn a policy that maximizes the expected cumulative reward over time.

Key Concepts:

1. **Agent:** The learner or decision-maker that interacts with the environment to achieve a goal.

2. **Environment:** The external system with which the agent interacts. It provides feedback to the agent based

on its actions.

3. **State:** A representation of the current situation or configuration of the environment.

4. **Action:** A decision or move made by the agent that affects the state of the environment.

5. **Reward:** A scalar feedback signal provided by the environment to indicate the immediate benefit or cost of the agent's action.

6. **Policy:** A mapping from states to actions that defines the agent's behavior. The policy can be deterministic or stochastic.

7. **Value Function:** A function that estimates the expected cumulative reward for a given state or state-action pair.

8. **Q-Function (Action-Value Function):** A function that estimates the expected cumulative reward for taking a specific action in a given state and following the policy thereafter.

9. **Discount Factor (γ):** A factor between 0 and 1 that determines the importance of future rewards. A discount factor close to 1 values future rewards highly, while a factor close to 0 emphasizes immediate rewards.

Reinforcement Learning Framework

1. **Markov Decision Process (MDP):**
   - **Definition:** A mathematical framework used to model decision-making problems in reinforcement learning. An MDP is defined by a tuple (S, A, P, R, γ), where:
     - S: A finite set of states.
     - A: A finite set of actions.
     - P: A state transition probability matrix, where $P(s'|s, a)$ represents the

probability of transitioning to state s' from state s after taking action a.

- R: A reward function, where R(s, a) represents the expected reward for taking action a in state s.
- γ: The discount factor.

2. **Exploration vs. Exploitation:**

   - **Definition:** The trade-off between exploring new actions to discover their rewards (exploration) and choosing the best-known action to maximize cumulative rewards (exploitation).

   - **Strategies:** Common exploration strategies include ε-greedy (choosing a random action with probability ε) and softmax (sampling actions based on a probability distribution).

Key Reinforcement Learning Algorithms

1. **Q-Learning:**

   - **Definition:** A model-free, off-policy algorithm that learns the optimal Q-function (action-value function) by updating Q-values using the Bellman equation.

   - **Update Rule:** $Q(s, a) \leftarrow Q(s, a) + \alpha [r + \gamma \max Q(s', a') - Q(s, a)]$, where α is the learning rate, r is the reward, and s' and a' are the next state and action.

   - **Advantages:** Simple and effective for discrete action spaces.

   - **Limitations:** May struggle with large or continuous state-action spaces.

2. **SARSA (State-Action-Reward-State-Action):**

   - **Definition:** A model-free, on-policy algorithm that updates Q-values based on the actions taken by the current policy.

- **Update Rule:** $Q(s, a) \leftarrow Q(s, a) + \alpha [r + \gamma Q(s', a') - Q(s, a)]$, where α is the learning rate, r is the reward, and s' and a' are the next state and action.
- **Advantages:** Incorporates the policy being followed, leading to more stable learning.
- **Limitations:** May converge more slowly than Q-learning.

3. **Deep Q-Network (DQN):**

- **Definition:** An extension of Q-learning that uses deep neural networks to approximate the Q-function, enabling RL to handle high-dimensional state spaces.
- **Key Components:** Experience replay (storing and sampling past experiences) and target networks (stabilizing training by using a separate network for target Q-values).
- **Advantages:** Effective for complex problems like playing Atari games.
- **Limitations:** Computationally intensive and requires careful tuning of hyperparameters.

4. **Policy Gradient Methods:**

- **Definition:** A class of algorithms that optimize the policy directly by maximizing the expected cumulative reward using gradient ascent.
- **Key Concepts:** REINFORCE (Monte Carlo policy gradient) and actor-critic methods (combining value function and policy gradient).
- **Advantages:** Suitable for continuous action spaces and handling stochastic policies.

  ◦ **Limitations:** High variance in gradient estimates, leading to unstable learning.

5. **Proximal Policy Optimization (PPO):**

  ◦ **Definition:** An advanced policy gradient algorithm that improves stability by optimizing a clipped surrogate objective function.

  ◦ **Key Concepts:** Importance sampling, clipped objective function, and advantage estimation.

  ◦ **Advantages:** Stable and efficient, widely used in practice.

  ◦ **Limitations:** Requires careful tuning of hyperparameters.

Applications of Reinforcement Learning

1. **Game Playing:**

  ◦ **Description:** RL has achieved remarkable success in training agents to play and master complex games.

  ◦ **Use Case:** AlphaGo (playing Go), AlphaZero (playing chess and shogi), DQN (playing Atari games).

2. **Robotics:**

  ◦ **Description:** RL enables robots to learn and adapt to dynamic environments, performing tasks such as manipulation, navigation, and locomotion.

  ◦ **Use Case:** Robotic grasping, autonomous drone navigation, legged locomotion.

3. **Autonomous Vehicles:**

  ◦ **Description:** RL is used to train autonomous vehicles to navigate and make decisions in complex traffic environments.

- **Use Case:** Self-driving cars, autonomous drones, delivery robots.

4. **Recommendation Systems:**

    - **Description:** RL enhances recommendation systems by personalizing content and optimizing long-term user engagement.
    - **Use Case:** Movie and music recommendations, personalized news feeds, e-commerce product recommendations.

5. **Finance:**

    - **Description:** RL is applied to optimize trading strategies, portfolio management, and financial decision-making.
    - **Use Case:** Algorithmic trading, portfolio optimization, risk management.

6. **Healthcare:**

    - **Description:** RL is used to optimize treatment plans, drug discovery, and personalized medicine.
    - **Use Case:** Optimizing chemotherapy schedules, discovering new drugs, personalizing treatment plans.

7. **Industrial Automation:**

    - **Description:** RL improves industrial processes by optimizing resource allocation, production schedules, and maintenance strategies.
    - **Use Case:** Optimizing manufacturing processes, predictive maintenance, supply chain management.

Practical Example: Building a Simple Q-Learning Agent Environment:

- We will use the OpenAI Gym environment "FrozenLake," where the agent must navigate a grid to reach a goal while avoiding holes.

Steps:

1. **Environment Setup:**
   - Load and initialize the FrozenLake environment from OpenAI Gym.

2. **Q-Table Initialization:**
   - Initialize a Q-table with all zeros, where rows represent states and columns represent actions.

3. **Q-Learning Algorithm:**
   - Implement the Q-learning algorithm to update the Q-values based on the agent's actions and rewards.

4. **Training:**
   - Train the Q-learning agent for a specified number of episodes, updating the Q-values and policy.

5. **Evaluation:**
   - Evaluate the trained agent by testing its performance in the environment.

Sample Code (using OpenAI Gym and NumPy):

python
```
import gym
import numpy as np

# Load the FrozenLake environment
env = gym.make("FrozenLake-v0")

# Initialize the Q-table
num_states = env.observation_space.n
num_actions = env.action_space.n
Q = np.zeros((num_states, num_actions))

# Set the hyperparameters
```

```
alpha = 0.1  # Learning rate
gamma = 0.99  # Discount factor
epsilon = 0.1  # Exploration rate
num_episodes = 1000

# Q-learning algorithm
for episode in range(num_episodes):
    state = env.reset()
    done = False
    while not done:
        # Choose an action (epsilon-greedy policy)
        if np.random.rand() < epsilon:
            action = env.action_space.sample()
        else:
            action = np.argmax(Q[state])

        # Take the action and observe the next state and reward
        next_state, reward, done, _ = env.step(action)

        # Update the Q-value
        Q[state, action] = Q[state, action] + alpha * (reward + gamma *
np.max(Q[next_state]) - Q[state, action])

        # Move to the next state
        state = next_state

# Evaluate the trained agent
total_rewards = 0
for episode in range(100):
    state = env.reset()
    done = False
    while not done:
        action = np.argmax(Q[state])
        next_state, reward, done, _ =
```

CHAPTER 19: AI
IN ROBOTICS

Overview

AI in robotics represents the fusion of artificial intelligence and robotics, enabling robots to perform tasks autonomously, adapt to dynamic environments, and interact with humans in meaningful ways. This chapter explores the integration of AI and robotics, key components and technologies, practical applications, and challenges. By understanding these concepts, you will gain insights into how AI is revolutionizing the field of robotics, enhancing capabilities, and enabling new possibilities.

Integration of AI and Robotics

Definition: AI in robotics involves embedding intelligent algorithms and models into robotic systems to enable them to perceive, reason, learn, and make decisions. This integration allows robots to operate autonomously and adapt to changing conditions.

Key Components:

1. **Sensors:**
   - **Function:** Sensors provide robots with the ability to perceive their environment. Common sensors include cameras, LiDAR, ultrasonic sensors, and accelerometers.
   - **Applications:** Object detection, obstacle avoidance, environmental mapping.

2. **Actuators:**

- **Function:** Actuators are responsible for executing actions and movements. They convert electrical signals into mechanical motion.
- **Applications:** Robotic arms, wheels, legs, grippers.

3. **Control Systems:**

- **Function:** Control systems manage the robot's movements and ensure accurate execution of tasks. They process sensor data and generate control signals for actuators.
- **Applications:** Path planning, motion control, feedback loops.

4. **Algorithms:**

- **Function:** AI algorithms enable robots to make decisions, learn from experiences, and adapt to new situations. Common algorithms include machine learning, deep learning, and reinforcement learning.
- **Applications:** Autonomous navigation, manipulation, human-robot interaction.

Key Technologies in AI Robotics

1. **Computer Vision:**

- **Definition:** Computer vision enables robots to interpret and understand visual information from cameras and other sensors.
- **Techniques:** Image recognition, object detection, image segmentation, SLAM (Simultaneous Localization and Mapping).
- **Applications:** Autonomous vehicles, industrial inspection, medical imaging.

2. **Natural Language Processing (NLP):**

- **Definition:** NLP allows robots to understand

and generate human language, enabling communication with humans.

- **Techniques:** Speech recognition, language understanding, dialogue systems.
- **Applications:** Voice-activated assistants, customer service robots, interactive toys.

3. **Reinforcement Learning:**

- **Definition:** Reinforcement learning enables robots to learn optimal actions through trial and error by receiving feedback from the environment.
- **Techniques:** Q-learning, deep Q-networks (DQN), policy gradient methods.
- **Applications:** Robot navigation, manipulation, game playing.

4. **Motion Planning:**

- **Definition:** Motion planning involves generating a sequence of movements for a robot to achieve a specific goal while avoiding obstacles.
- **Techniques:** A*, RRT (Rapidly-exploring Random Tree), Dijkstra's algorithm.
- **Applications:** Autonomous driving, robotic arms, drones.

Practical Applications of AI in Robotics

1. **Industrial Automation:**

- **Description:** AI-powered robots automate repetitive and hazardous tasks in manufacturing, improving efficiency and safety.
- **Use Case:** Assembly line robots, quality inspection, material handling.

2. **Healthcare and Medical Robotics:**

- **Description:** AI-enabled robots assist in medical procedures, patient care, and rehabilitation.
- **Use Case:** Surgical robots, robotic prosthetics, telemedicine robots.

3. **Autonomous Vehicles:**
   - **Description:** AI drives the development of autonomous vehicles that can navigate and operate without human intervention.
   - **Use Case:** Self-driving cars, delivery drones, autonomous shuttles.

4. **Service and Hospitality:**
   - **Description:** Service robots equipped with AI enhance customer experiences in hospitality and retail environments.
   - **Use Case:** Concierge robots, robotic waiters, inventory management.

5. **Agriculture:**
   - **Description:** AI-powered robots optimize agricultural practices, increasing productivity and sustainability.
   - **Use Case:** Automated planting, crop monitoring, harvesting robots.

6. **Space Exploration:**
   - **Description:** AI enhances the capabilities of robots used in space exploration, enabling them to operate in challenging environments.
   - **Use Case:** Mars rovers, robotic arms on space stations, planetary exploration.

7. **Disaster Response:**
   - **Description:** AI-driven robots assist in disaster response and recovery efforts,

performing tasks that are dangerous for humans.

- **Use Case:** Search and rescue robots, firefighting robots, hazardous material handling.

Challenges in AI Robotics

1. **Perception and Understanding:**

   - **Description:** Robots must accurately perceive and understand their environment to make informed decisions.
   - **Solution:** Use advanced sensors, sensor fusion techniques, and robust computer vision algorithms.

2. **Learning and Adaptation:**

   - **Description:** Robots need to learn from experiences and adapt to new situations in dynamic environments.
   - **Solution:** Implement reinforcement learning, transfer learning, and continuous learning algorithms.

3. **Human-Robot Interaction:**

   - **Description:** Ensuring safe and effective interaction between robots and humans is critical.
   - **Solution:** Develop intuitive interfaces, natural language processing, and safety protocols.

4. **Robustness and Reliability:**

   - **Description:** Robots must operate reliably under various conditions and handle uncertainties.
   - **Solution:** Design robust control systems, fault-tolerant algorithms, and real-time monitoring.

5. **Ethical and Social Implications:**
   - **Description:** The deployment of AI robots raises ethical and social concerns, such as job displacement and privacy.
   - **Solution:** Establish ethical guidelines, ensure transparency, and promote responsible AI development.
6. **Energy Efficiency:**
   - **Description:** Robots require efficient energy management to operate for extended periods.
   - **Solution:** Use energy-efficient actuators, optimize power consumption, and develop advanced battery technologies.

Practical Example: Building a Simple Robot Navigation System

Objective:
- Develop a robot navigation system that can navigate through a maze using reinforcement learning.

Environment:
- We will use a simulated maze environment where the robot receives rewards for reaching the goal and penalties for hitting obstacles.

Steps:
1. **Environment Setup:**
   - Create a simulated maze environment with defined states, actions, rewards, and penalties.
2. **Q-Learning Algorithm:**
   - Implement the Q-learning algorithm to update the Q-values based on the robot's actions and rewards.
3. **Training:**
   - Train the robot to navigate through the maze for a specified number of episodes, updating

the Q-values and policy.

4. **Evaluation:**

- Evaluate the trained robot by testing its performance in the maze environment.

Sample Code (using NumPy):

python

```python
import numpy as np

# Define the maze environment
maze = np.array([
    [0, 0, 0, 1, 0],
    [1, 1, 0, 1, 0],
    [0, 0, 0, 0, 0],
    [0, 1, 1, 1, 0],
    [0, 0, 0, 0, 2]
])

# Define the actions: up, down, left, right
actions = [(0, -1), (0, 1), (-1, 0), (1, 0)]

# Initialize the Q-table
num_states = maze.size
num_actions = len(actions)
Q = np.zeros((num_states, num_actions))

# Set the hyperparameters
alpha = 0.1  # Learning rate
gamma = 0.99  # Discount factor
epsilon = 0.1  # Exploration rate
num_episodes = 1000

# Define the rewards
goal_reward = 10
collision_penalty = -1
step_penalty = -0.1

# Q-learning algorithm
for episode in range(num_episodes):
    # Initialize the robot's starting position
    state = np.unravel_index(np.argwhere(maze == 0)[0], maze.shape)
    done = False

    while not done:
        # Choose an action (epsilon-greedy policy)
```

```python
if np.random.rand() < epsilon:
    action = np.random.choice(range(num_actions))
else:
    action = np.argmax(Q[np.ravel_multi_index(state, maze.shape)])

# Take the action and observe the next state and reward
next_state = (state[0] + actions[action][0], state[1] + actions[action][1])

if (0 <= next_state[0] < maze.shape[0] and
        0 <= next_state[1] < maze.shape[1] and
        maze[next_state] != 1):
    reward = step_penalty

    if maze[next_state] == 2:
        reward = goal_reward
        done = True
else:
    next_state = state
    reward = collision_penalty

# Update the Q-value
Q[np.ravel_multi_index(state,         maze.shape),         action]         =
Q[np.ravel_multi_index(state, maze.shape), action] + alpha * (
        reward + gamma * np.max(Q[np.ravel_multi_index(next_state,
maze.shape)]) - Q[np.ravel_multi_index(state, maze.shape), action])

# Move to the next state
state = next_state

# Evaluate the trained robot
total_rewards = 0
for episode in range(100):
    state = np.unravel_index(np.argwhere(maze == 0)[0], maze.shape)
    done = False
    while not done:
        action = np.argmax(Q[np.ravel_multi_index(state, maze.shape)])
        next
```

CHAPTER 20:
EXPLAINABLE AI (XAI)

Overview

As artificial intelligence (AI) systems become increasingly integrated into various aspects of our lives, the need for explainability and transparency in AI decisions has become more critical. Explainable AI (XAI) aims to make the decision-making processes of AI systems understandable and interpretable to humans. This chapter explores the importance of explainability in AI, key techniques and methods for achieving explainability, practical applications, and the challenges associated with explainable AI.

Importance of Explainable AI

1. **Trust and Transparency:**

   ◦ Explainability enhances trust in AI systems by providing insights into how decisions are made. Transparent AI systems are more likely to be trusted by users, stakeholders, and regulators.

2. **Accountability:**

   ◦ Explainable AI enables accountability by allowing stakeholders to understand and evaluate the rationale behind AI decisions. This is crucial in scenarios where AI decisions have significant consequences, such as healthcare, finance, and criminal justice.

3. **Compliance with Regulations:**

- Regulatory frameworks, such as the European Union's General Data Protection Regulation (GDPR), emphasize the need for explainability in AI systems. Compliance with these regulations requires AI systems to provide clear and understandable explanations for their decisions.

4. **Improved Decision-Making:**

- Explainable AI aids human decision-makers by providing insights and justifications for AI recommendations. This can lead to more informed and confident decision-making.

5. **Debugging and Improving AI Models:**

- Understanding the decision-making process of AI models helps identify errors, biases, and areas for improvement. This is essential for refining and optimizing AI systems.

Key Techniques and Methods for Explainable AI

1. **Model-Agnostic Methods:**

- Model-agnostic methods can be applied to any AI model, regardless of its architecture. These methods treat the AI model as a black box and focus on interpreting its input-output behavior.

LIME (Local Interpretable Model-agnostic Explanations):

- **Description:** LIME approximates the decision boundary of a black-box model locally around a specific prediction by fitting an interpretable model (e.g., linear model) to the perturbed data.

- **Use Case:** Explaining individual predictions of complex models like neural networks and ensemble methods.

SHAP (SHapley Additive exPlanations):

- **Description:** SHAP assigns each feature an importance value based on Shapley values from cooperative game theory. It explains the contribution of each feature to the model's predictions.
- **Use Case:** Providing global and local explanations for any machine learning model.

Partial Dependence Plots (PDPs):

- **Description:** PDPs show the relationship between a feature and the predicted outcome by averaging the model's predictions over the distribution of other features.
- **Use Case:** Visualizing the impact of individual features on the model's predictions.

2. **Intrinsic Interpretability:**

- Intrinsic interpretability refers to the inherent transparency of certain AI models. These models are designed to be interpretable by humans without requiring additional methods.

Decision Trees:

- **Description:** Decision trees use a tree-like structure to represent decisions and their possible consequences. Each path from the root to a leaf represents a decision rule.
- **Use Case:** Explaining decisions in classification and regression tasks.

Linear Models:

- **Description:** Linear models, such as linear regression and logistic regression, provide clear and interpretable relationships between features and the predicted outcome.
- **Use Case:** Explaining predictions in tasks where

linear relationships exist between features and the target.

Rule-Based Models:

- **Description:** Rule-based models, such as decision rules and association rules, use logical rules to make decisions. These rules are easy to understand and interpret.
- **Use Case:** Explaining decisions in tasks where clear and concise rules can be extracted from the data.

3. **Post-Hoc Explanations:**

- Post-hoc explanations are generated after the AI model has been trained. These methods aim to provide insights into the model's behavior without altering its architecture.

Feature Importance:

- **Description:** Feature importance measures the contribution of each feature to the model's predictions. Common methods include permutation importance and feature importance from tree-based models.
- **Use Case:** Identifying the most influential features in the model.

Counterfactual Explanations:

- **Description:** Counterfactual explanations provide alternative scenarios that would change the model's prediction. They help users understand what changes in the input would lead to different outcomes.
- **Use Case:** Explaining individual predictions and providing actionable insights.

Surrogate Models:

- **Description:** Surrogate models are interpretable

models (e.g., decision trees) trained to approximate the predictions of a complex black-box model. They provide insights into the model's behavior.

- **Use Case:** Explaining complex models by using simpler, interpretable models.

Practical Applications of Explainable AI

1. **Healthcare:**
   - **Description:** Explainable AI is crucial in healthcare to ensure that AI-driven diagnoses and treatment recommendations are transparent and understandable to medical professionals and patients.
   - **Use Case:** Explaining the rationale behind AI-generated medical diagnoses, predicting disease risk factors.

2. **Finance:**
   - **Description:** In the financial sector, explainable AI helps build trust in automated decision-making systems, such as credit scoring and fraud detection.
   - **Use Case:** Explaining credit approval decisions, identifying factors contributing to fraud detection.

3. **Criminal Justice:**
   - **Description:** Explainable AI ensures transparency and accountability in AI-driven decisions related to sentencing, parole, and risk assessment.
   - **Use Case:** Providing explanations for risk assessment scores, ensuring fairness in sentencing decisions.

4. **Human Resources:**

- **Description:** Explainable AI assists in recruitment and employee evaluation by providing transparent insights into AI-driven hiring and performance assessment decisions.
- **Use Case:** Explaining candidate ranking decisions, identifying factors influencing performance evaluations.

5. **Autonomous Vehicles:**

- **Description:** Explainable AI enhances the safety and reliability of autonomous vehicles by providing insights into the decision-making processes of AI-driven systems.
- **Use Case:** Explaining decisions related to obstacle avoidance, route planning, and emergency braking.

6. **Customer Support:**

- **Description:** Explainable AI improves customer support by providing transparent and understandable responses generated by AI-powered chatbots and virtual assistants.
- **Use Case:** Explaining the reasoning behind responses to customer queries, ensuring consistency in support interactions.

Challenges in Explainable AI

1. **Trade-Off Between Accuracy and Interpretability:**

- **Description:** Complex models often achieve higher accuracy but are less interpretable, while simpler models are more interpretable but may have lower accuracy.
- **Solution:** Balance the trade-off by using hybrid approaches that combine interpretable models with complex models.

2. Scalability:

- ◦ **Description:** Generating explanations for large and complex models can be computationally intensive and time-consuming.
- ◦ **Solution:** Use efficient algorithms and techniques to scale explainable AI methods to large datasets and models.

3. Consistency of Explanations:

- ◦ **Description:** Ensuring that explanations are consistent and reliable across different instances and scenarios can be challenging.
- ◦ **Solution:** Validate explanations through human feedback and robustness testing.

4. Interpretation of Explanations:

- ◦ **Description:** Users may find it difficult to understand and interpret the explanations provided by AI systems.
- ◦ **Solution:** Present explanations in a user-friendly and contextually relevant manner, tailored to the audience's expertise.

5. Ethical and Privacy Concerns:

- ◦ **Description:** Ensuring that explainable AI methods do not compromise user privacy or introduce biases is critical.
- ◦ **Solution:** Implement ethical guidelines, data privacy policies, and bias mitigation techniques.

Practical Example: Using LIME for Explainable AI

Objective:

- • Use LIME (Local Interpretable Model-agnostic Explanations) to explain the predictions of a black-box model on a classification task.

Dataset:

- We will use the UCI Iris dataset, which contains measurements of iris flowers and their species.

Steps:

1. **Data Preparation:**
   - Load and preprocess the Iris dataset (e.g., normalization, splitting into training and testing sets).

2. **Model Training:**
   - Train a black-box model (e.g., random forest classifier) on the training data.

3. **LIME Explanation:**
   - Use LIME to generate explanations for the model's predictions on individual instances.

4. **Evaluation:**
   - Evaluate the interpretability and usefulness of the explanations.

Sample Code (using scikit-learn and LIME):

python

```
import numpy as np
import pandas as pd
from sklearn.datasets import load_iris
from sklearn.model_selection import train_test_split
from sklearn.ensemble import RandomForestClassifier
import lime
import lime.lime_tabular

# Load and preprocess the Iris dataset
iris = load_iris()
X = iris.data
y = iris.target
X_train, X_test, y_train, y_test = train_test_split(X, y, test_size=0.2,
random_state=42)

# Train a random forest classifier
model = RandomForestClassifier(n_estimators=100, random_state=42)
model.fit(X_train, y_train)
```

```
# Initialize LIME explainer
explainer = lime.lime_tabular.LimeTabularExplainer(X_train,
feature_names=iris.feature_names, class_names=iris.target_names,
discretize_continuous=True)

# Select an instance to explain
instance = X_test[0]
```

CHAPTER 21: AI PROJECT LIFECYCLE

Overview

The AI project lifecycle encompasses the stages involved in planning, developing, deploying, and maintaining AI systems. It provides a structured approach to managing AI projects, ensuring they are delivered successfully and meet business objectives. This chapter explores the key stages of the AI project lifecycle, including project planning, data collection and preparation, model development, deployment, monitoring, and best practices for managing AI projects effectively.

Stages of an AI Project

1. **Project Planning:**
   - **Objectives and Scope:** Define the project's objectives, scope, and expected outcomes. Identify the problem to be solved and the business value to be derived from the AI system.
   - **Stakeholder Identification:** Identify and engage key stakeholders, including business leaders, data scientists, engineers, and end-users. Ensure their needs and expectations are considered.
   - **Resource Allocation:** Allocate necessary resources, including budget, personnel, hardware, and software. Develop a project timeline with clear milestones and

deliverables.

- **Risk Assessment:** Identify potential risks and challenges, such as data quality issues, technical limitations, and ethical concerns. Develop mitigation strategies to address these risks.

2. **Data Collection and Preparation:**

- **Data Collection:** Gather relevant data from various sources, such as databases, sensors, APIs, and external datasets. Ensure the data is representative of the problem domain.

- **Data Cleaning:** Clean the data to remove noise, handle missing values, and correct inconsistencies. This step is crucial for ensuring data quality and reliability.

- **Data Transformation:** Transform the data into a suitable format for analysis, including normalization, encoding categorical variables, and feature engineering.

- **Data Splitting:** Split the data into training, validation, and testing sets to evaluate model performance and prevent overfitting.

3. **Model Development:**

- **Algorithm Selection:** Select appropriate algorithms based on the problem type, data characteristics, and desired outcomes. Consider both traditional machine learning and deep learning algorithms.

- **Model Training:** Train the selected models using the training dataset. Use techniques such as cross-validation and hyperparameter tuning to optimize model performance.

- **Model Evaluation:** Evaluate the trained models using the validation and testing datasets. Use relevant metrics, such as accuracy, precision, recall, and F1 score, to assess performance.

- **Model Selection:** Select the best-performing model based on evaluation results. Consider both performance metrics and interpretability.

4. **Deployment:**

- **Deployment Strategy:** Develop a deployment strategy that considers factors such as scalability, reliability, and integration with existing systems. Choose between cloud, on-premises, or hybrid deployment.

- **Model Export:** Export the trained model in a suitable format for deployment, such as ONNX, TensorFlow SavedModel, or PyTorch ScriptModule.

- **API Development:** Develop APIs or microservices to expose the model's functionality to end-users or other systems. Ensure the APIs are secure, efficient, and well-documented.

- **Integration:** Integrate the deployed model with existing applications, workflows, or systems. Ensure seamless communication and data exchange between components.

5. **Monitoring and Maintenance:**

- **Performance Monitoring:** Continuously monitor the model's performance in production. Track key metrics, such as latency, throughput, and accuracy, to ensure the model meets performance requirements.

- **Drift Detection:** Detect data drift and model drift by comparing current data distributions and model predictions with historical trends. Implement strategies to address drift, such as retraining or updating the model.

- **Maintenance:** Regularly update and maintain the model to address changes in data, requirements, or system environments. Implement a versioning system to manage updates and rollback changes if needed.
- **Feedback Loop:** Collect feedback from end-users and stakeholders to identify areas for improvement. Use this feedback to refine the model and enhance its performance.

6. **Documentation and Reporting:**

- **Documentation:** Document all stages of the AI project, including data sources, preprocessing steps, model architecture, training procedures, and evaluation results. Ensure documentation is clear, comprehensive, and accessible.
- **Reporting:** Generate reports to communicate project progress, outcomes, and insights to stakeholders. Use visualizations and metrics to convey key findings effectively.

Best Practices for Managing AI Projects

1. **Collaborative Teamwork:**

- Foster collaboration between data scientists, engineers, domain experts, and business stakeholders. Encourage open communication, knowledge sharing, and cross-functional teamwork.

2. **Agile Methodology:**

- Adopt agile methodologies, such as Scrum or Kanban, to manage AI projects. Use iterative development, continuous feedback, and flexible planning to adapt to changing requirements.

3. **Ethical Considerations:**
   - Ensure ethical considerations are integrated into the project lifecycle. Address issues such as bias, fairness, transparency, and privacy. Develop ethical guidelines and conduct regular ethical reviews.

4. **Scalability and Robustness:**
   - Design AI systems with scalability and robustness in mind. Use scalable infrastructure, parallel processing, and fault-tolerant designs to handle large datasets and high-demand scenarios.

5. **Continuous Learning and Improvement:**
   - Encourage continuous learning and improvement within the team. Stay updated with the latest advancements in AI, machine learning, and data science. Implement regular training sessions and knowledge-sharing initiatives.

6. **User-Centric Design:**
   - Prioritize user-centric design by involving end-users in the development process. Gather user feedback, conduct usability testing, and ensure the AI system meets user needs and expectations.

Conclusion

The AI project lifecycle provides a structured approach to managing AI projects, ensuring they are delivered successfully and meet business objectives. In this chapter, we explored the key stages of the AI project lifecycle, including project planning, data collection and preparation, model development, deployment, monitoring, and maintenance. We also discussed best practices for managing AI projects effectively, such as collaborative teamwork, agile methodology, ethical considerations, scalability, continuous learning, and user-centric design.

By following these principles and practices, you can successfully manage AI projects and deliver impactful AI solutions. As we continue our journey through the subsequent chapters, we will delve deeper into specific aspects of AI implementation and deployment, providing practical insights and guidance.

In the next chapter, we will explore data collection and management, discussing techniques for gathering, storing, and managing data for AI projects. We will also address data privacy and security considerations.

CHAPTER 22: DATA COLLECTION AND MANAGEMENT

Overview

Data is the backbone of any AI project. The quality and quantity of data significantly impact the performance of AI models. Effective data collection and management are crucial for ensuring that AI systems are accurate, reliable, and ethical. This chapter explores techniques for gathering, storing, and managing data for AI projects, and addresses data privacy and security considerations.

Data Sources and Collection Methods

Data Sources:

1. **Internal Data:**
   - **Description:** Data generated within an organization, such as customer transactions, sales records, and operational data.
   - **Examples:** CRM data, ERP systems, website analytics, internal surveys.

2. **External Data:**
   - **Description:** Data obtained from external sources, such as third-party providers, public datasets, and social media.
   - **Examples:** Government databases, market research reports, social media feeds, APIs.

3. **Generated Data:**

   - **Description:** Data created specifically for training AI models, such as synthetic data and simulated environments.
   - **Examples:** Synthetic images, simulated sensor data, generated text.

Data Collection Methods:

1. **Manual Data Collection:**

   - **Description:** Collecting data manually through surveys, interviews, and observations.
   - **Advantages:** High accuracy and control over data quality.
   - **Disadvantages:** Time-consuming and labor-intensive.

2. **Automated Data Collection:**

   - **Description:** Using automated tools and technologies to gather data from various sources.
   - **Advantages:** Efficient and scalable, real-time data collection.
   - **Disadvantages:** May require technical expertise and infrastructure.

3. **Web Scraping:**

   - **Description:** Extracting data from websites using automated scripts and tools.
   - **Advantages:** Access to a vast amount of data available on the web.
   - **Disadvantages:** Legal and ethical considerations, potential for data quality issues.

4. **APIs (Application Programming Interfaces):**

- **Description:** Using APIs to access and retrieve data from external systems and services.
- **Advantages:** Reliable and structured data, real-time updates.
- **Disadvantages:** Dependency on third-party providers, potential costs.

5. **Sensors and IoT Devices:**

- **Description:** Collecting data from sensors and Internet of Things (IoT) devices deployed in the environment.
- **Advantages:** Real-time and continuous data collection, relevant for specific applications.
- **Disadvantages:** Requires infrastructure setup and maintenance, potential data privacy concerns.

Data Storage and Management Solutions

1. **Databases:**

- **Relational Databases:**
  - **Description:** Structured databases that store data in tables with predefined schemas.
  - **Examples:** MySQL, PostgreSQL, Microsoft SQL Server.
  - **Advantages:** Strong consistency, support for complex queries, well-established technology.
  - **Disadvantages:** Less flexible for unstructured data, may require schema design and maintenance.
- **NoSQL Databases:**
  - **Description:** Non-relational databases that store data in various formats, such as key-value pairs, documents,

and graphs.

- **Examples:** MongoDB, Cassandra, Redis.
- **Advantages:** Flexible and scalable, suitable for unstructured and semi-structured data.
- **Disadvantages:** May lack strong consistency, limited support for complex queries.

2. **Data Lakes:**

   - **Description:** Centralized repositories that store raw and unprocessed data in its native format.
   - **Examples:** AWS Lake Formation, Azure Data Lake, Google Cloud Storage.
   - **Advantages:** Scalability, flexibility, support for various data types.
   - **Disadvantages:** Requires proper data governance and management to avoid data swamp.

3. **Data Warehouses:**

   - **Description:** Structured and optimized storage solutions for analytical and reporting purposes.
   - **Examples:** Amazon Redshift, Google BigQuery, Snowflake.
   - **Advantages:** Optimized for querying and analysis, supports large-scale data processing.
   - **Disadvantages:** May require ETL (Extract, Transform, Load) processes, higher costs for storage and processing.

4. **Cloud Storage:**

   - **Description:** Using cloud-based storage

services to store and manage data.

- **Examples:** Amazon S3, Google Cloud Storage, Microsoft Azure Blob Storage.
- **Advantages:** Scalability, reliability, accessibility, cost-effective.
- **Disadvantages:** Dependency on cloud providers, potential data privacy concerns.

Data Preprocessing and Transformation

1. **Data Cleaning:**
   - **Description:** Removing or correcting errors, inconsistencies, and missing values in the data.
   - **Techniques:** Imputation, outlier detection, data deduplication, normalization.

2. **Data Transformation:**
   - **Description:** Converting data into a suitable format for analysis and modeling.
   - **Techniques:** Scaling, encoding categorical variables, feature engineering, aggregation.

3. **Data Integration:**
   - **Description:** Combining data from multiple sources to create a unified dataset.
   - **Techniques:** Data merging, joining, alignment, resolving conflicts.

4. **Data Anonymization:**
   - **Description:** Removing or masking personally identifiable information (PII) to protect privacy.
   - **Techniques:** Data masking, pseudonymization, generalization, k-anonymity.

Data Privacy and Security Considerations

1. **Data Privacy:**
   - **Definition:** Ensuring that data collection, storage, and processing comply with privacy regulations and protect individuals' rights.
   - **Key Regulations:**
     - **GDPR (General Data Protection Regulation):** A regulation in the European Union that governs data protection and privacy for individuals.
     - **CCPA (California Consumer Privacy Act):** A regulation in California that provides privacy rights and protections for consumers.
   - **Best Practices:**
     - **Data Minimization:** Collect and store only the data necessary for the intended purpose.
     - **Consent:** Obtain informed consent from individuals before collecting and processing their data.
     - **Transparency:** Provide clear information about data collection, usage, and sharing practices.

2. **Data Security:**
   - **Definition:** Protecting data from unauthorized access, breaches, and other security threats.
   - **Key Practices:**
     - **Encryption:** Use encryption techniques to protect data at rest and in transit.
     - **Access Control:** Implement strict access control measures to limit data

access to authorized personnel only.

- **Regular Audits:** Conduct regular security audits and assessments to identify and address vulnerabilities.
- **Backup and Recovery:** Implement backup and disaster recovery plans to ensure data availability and integrity.

Data Governance

1. **Definition:**
   - Data governance involves establishing policies, procedures, and standards for managing data within an organization. It ensures data quality, integrity, and compliance with regulations.

2. **Key Components:**
   - **Data Stewardship:** Assigning roles and responsibilities for data management, including data owners, stewards, and custodians.
   - **Data Quality Management:** Implementing processes to monitor and improve data quality, including data profiling, validation, and cleansing.
   - **Metadata Management:** Managing metadata to provide context and understanding of data, including data dictionaries, catalogs, and lineage.
   - **Data Policies and Standards:** Developing and enforcing data policies and standards to ensure consistency, accuracy, and compliance.

Conclusion

Effective data collection and management are critical for the success of AI projects. In this chapter, we explored various data sources and collection methods, data storage and management solutions, data preprocessing and transformation techniques, and data privacy and security considerations. We also discussed the importance of data governance in ensuring data quality, integrity, and compliance with regulations.

By implementing best practices for data collection and management, organizations can ensure that their AI systems are built on a solid foundation of high-quality data. As we continue our journey through the subsequent chapters, we will delve deeper into specific aspects of AI implementation and deployment, providing practical insights and guidance.

In the next chapter, we will explore model training and optimization techniques, discussing strategies for training AI models effectively and optimizing their performance. We will also address common challenges and solutions in the model training process.

CHAPTER 23: MODEL TRAINING AND OPTIMIZATION

Overview

Model training and optimization are critical steps in the development of AI systems. Effective training ensures that models learn to make accurate predictions, while optimization techniques enhance their performance and efficiency. This chapter explores strategies for training AI models, including data preprocessing, hyperparameter tuning, and regularization. We also address common challenges and solutions in the model training process, providing practical insights to help you develop robust and high-performing AI models.

Techniques for Effective Model Training

1. **Data Preprocessing:**

   ○ **Normalization and Scaling:**

     ▪ Normalization scales the data to a range of [0, 1] or [-1, 1], ensuring that features with different scales do not disproportionately influence the model.

     ▪ Standardization transforms the data to have a mean of 0 and a standard deviation of 1, which is particularly useful for algorithms that assume normally distributed data.

- **Example:** In Python, you can use StandardScaler and MinMaxScaler from the sklearn.preprocessing module.
  - **Handling Missing Values:**
    - Imputation replaces missing values with estimated values, such as the mean, median, or mode of the feature.
    - Dropping rows or columns with missing values is another approach, although it can lead to a loss of data.
    - **Example:** In Python, you can use SimpleImputer from the sklearn.impute module.
  - **Encoding Categorical Variables:**
    - One-hot encoding converts categorical variables into binary vectors, where each category is represented by a unique binary code.
    - Label encoding assigns a unique integer to each category, which can be useful for ordinal variables.
    - **Example:** In Python, you can use OneHotEncoder and LabelEncoder from the sklearn.preprocessing module.
  - **Feature Engineering:**
    - Creating new features from existing data can enhance the model's ability to capture relevant patterns.
    - Techniques include polynomial features, interaction terms, and domain-specific transformations.
    - **Example:** In Python, you can use PolynomialFeatures from the

sklearn.preprocessing module.

2. **Hyperparameter Tuning:**
   ○ **Grid Search:**
     ▪ Grid search exhaustively searches over a specified set of hyperparameters to find the combination that yields the best model performance.
     ▪ **Example:** In Python, you can use GridSearchCV from the sklearn.model_selection module.
   ○ **Random Search:**
     ▪ Random search selects random combinations of hyperparameters to evaluate, which can be more efficient than grid search for large search spaces.
     ▪ **Example:** In Python, you can use RandomizedSearchCV from the sklearn.model_selection module.
   ○ **Bayesian Optimization:**
     ▪ Bayesian optimization models the objective function and uses it to select the next hyperparameters to evaluate, balancing exploration and exploitation.
     ▪ **Example:** Libraries like hyperopt and scikit-optimize provide implementations of Bayesian optimization.
   ○ **Automated Machine Learning (AutoML):**
     ▪ AutoML tools automate the process of hyperparameter tuning, model selection, and feature engineering, making it accessible to non-experts.

- **Example:** Tools like Auto-sklearn, TPOT, and H2O.ai provide AutoML solutions.

3. **Regularization:**
   ○ **L1 and L2 Regularization:**
     - L1 regularization (Lasso) adds a penalty equal to the absolute value of the coefficients, encouraging sparsity in the model.
     - L2 regularization (Ridge) adds a penalty equal to the squared value of the coefficients, preventing large coefficients.
     - **Example:** In Python, you can use Lasso and Ridge from the sklearn.linear_model module.
   ○ **Dropout:**
     - Dropout randomly sets a fraction of the input units to zero during training, preventing overfitting and improving generalization.
     - **Example:** In deep learning frameworks like TensorFlow and PyTorch, you can use Dropout layers.
   ○ **Early Stopping:**
     - Early stopping monitors the model's performance on a validation set and stops training when performance no longer improves, preventing overfitting.
     - **Example:** In Python, you can use EarlyStopping from the keras.callbacks module.

4. **Cross-Validation:**

- **K-Fold Cross-Validation:**
  - K-fold cross-validation splits the data into `k` folds, training the model on `k-1` folds and validating it on the remaining fold. This process is repeated `k` times, and the results are averaged.
  - **Example:** In Python, you can use `cross_val_score` from the `sklearn.model_selection` module.
- **Leave-One-Out Cross-Validation (LOOCV):**
  - LOOCV is a special case of k-fold cross-validation where `k` is equal to the number of samples. Each sample is used as a validation set exactly once.
  - **Example:** In Python, you can use `LeaveOneOut` from the `sklearn.model_selection` module.
- **Stratified Cross-Validation:**
  - Stratified cross-validation ensures that each fold has a similar distribution of classes, which is useful for imbalanced datasets.
  - **Example:** In Python, you can use `StratifiedKFold` from the `sklearn.model_selection` module.

Common Challenges and Solutions in Model Training

1. **Overfitting:**
   - **Description:** Overfitting occurs when a model learns the training data too well, including noise and outliers, leading to poor generalization to new data.
   - **Solutions:**

- Use regularization techniques, such as L1, L2, and dropout.
- Implement early stopping to prevent excessive training.
- Increase the size of the training dataset.

2. **Underfitting:**

   ◦ **Description:** Underfitting occurs when a model fails to capture the underlying patterns in the data, resulting in poor performance on both the training and testing sets.

   ◦ **Solutions:**

     - Increase model complexity by adding more features or using more sophisticated algorithms.
     - Improve feature engineering to enhance the model's ability to capture relevant patterns.
     - Reduce regularization strength to allow the model to fit the data better.

3. **Class Imbalance:**

   ◦ **Description:** Class imbalance occurs when the distribution of classes in the dataset is uneven, leading to biased model performance.

   ◦ **Solutions:**

     - Use resampling techniques, such as oversampling the minority class or undersampling the majority class.
     - Implement algorithms designed to handle imbalanced data, such as SMOTE (Synthetic Minority Over-sampling Technique).
     - Use performance metrics that account

for class imbalance, such as precision, recall, and F1 score.

4. **Data Leakage:**

- **Description:** Data leakage occurs when information from the test set inadvertently influences the training process, leading to overly optimistic performance estimates.

- **Solutions:**

  - Ensure proper separation of training, validation, and testing datasets.

  - Perform data preprocessing and feature engineering steps only on the training data, then apply them to the validation and test sets.

5. **Computational Complexity:**

- **Description:** Training complex models, especially deep learning models, can be computationally intensive and time-consuming.

- **Solutions:**

  - Use hardware acceleration, such as GPUs or TPUs, to speed up training.

  - Implement parallel processing and distributed computing techniques.

  - Optimize hyperparameters and reduce model complexity where possible.

6. **Interpretability:**

- **Description:** Complex models, such as deep learning networks, can be challenging to interpret and understand.

- **Solutions:**

  - Use model-agnostic interpretation techniques, such as LIME and SHAP.

- Implement interpretable models, such as decision trees and linear models, where possible.

Practical Example: Hyperparameter Tuning with Grid Search

Objective:

- Use grid search to optimize the hyperparameters of a Random Forest classifier on the Iris dataset.

Steps:

1. **Data Preparation:**
   - Load and preprocess the Iris dataset (e.g., normalization, splitting into training and testing sets).

2. **Model Initialization:**
   - Initialize a Random Forest classifier.

3. **Grid Search:**
   - Define the hyperparameter grid to search over, including the number of trees, maximum depth, and other relevant parameters.
   - Perform grid search to find the best hyperparameters.

4. **Evaluation:**
   - Evaluate the optimized model on the testing data using relevant metrics.

Sample Code (using scikit-learn):

python
```
import numpy as np
import pandas as pd
from sklearn.datasets import load_iris
from sklearn.model_selection import train_test_split, GridSearchCV
from sklearn.ensemble import RandomForestClassifier
from sklearn.metrics import accuracy_score

# Load and preprocess the Iris dataset
```

```python
iris = load_iris()
X = iris.data
y = iris.target
X_train, X_test, y_train, y_test = train_test_split(X, y, test_size=0.2,
random_state=42)

# Initialize a Random Forest classifier
model = RandomForestClassifier(random_state=42)

# Define the hyperparameter grid
param_grid = {
    'n_estimators': [50, 100, 150],
    'max_depth': [None, 10, 20],
    'min_samples_split': [2, 5, 10],
    'min_samples_leaf': [1, 2, 4]
}

# Perform grid search
grid_search = GridSearchCV(estimator=model, param_grid=param_grid
```

CHAPTER 24: AI DEPLOYMENT AND MONITORING

Overview

Once an AI model is trained and optimized, the next crucial step is to deploy it into a production environment where it can be used to make real-time predictions or decisions. Deployment involves integrating the model with existing systems, ensuring scalability and reliability, and continuously monitoring its performance to maintain accuracy and efficiency. This chapter explores the key aspects of AI deployment and monitoring, including deployment strategies, integration techniques, performance monitoring, and best practices for maintaining AI systems in production.

Deploying AI Models

1. **Deployment Strategies:**

   ○ **Batch Deployment:**

      ■ **Description:** Batch deployment involves processing large volumes of data at scheduled intervals. The model makes predictions on batches of data, which are then used for further analysis or reporting.

      ■ **Use Cases:** Financial forecasting, inventory management, customer segmentation.

- **Real-Time Deployment:**
  - **Description:** Real-time deployment enables the model to make predictions on individual data points as they are received. This approach is crucial for applications that require immediate responses.
  - **Use Cases:** Fraud detection, recommendation systems, autonomous vehicles.
- **Edge Deployment:**
  - **Description:** Edge deployment involves deploying models on edge devices, such as smartphones, IoT devices, or embedded systems. This approach reduces latency and allows for offline processing.
  - **Use Cases:** Augmented reality, smart home devices, industrial automation.
- **Cloud Deployment:**
  - **Description:** Cloud deployment leverages cloud infrastructure to host and manage AI models. It offers scalability, flexibility, and easy integration with other cloud services.
  - **Use Cases:** Web applications, SaaS platforms, large-scale data processing.

2. **Model Export and Serialization:**
   - **ONNX (Open Neural Network Exchange):**
     - **Description:** ONNX is an open standard for representing machine learning models. It enables interoperability between different

frameworks and platforms.

- **Use Cases:** Exporting models from frameworks like TensorFlow, PyTorch, and scikit-learn for deployment on various platforms.

○ **TensorFlow SavedModel:**

- **Description:** TensorFlow SavedModel is a format for saving TensorFlow models that includes both the architecture and weights.

- **Use Cases:** Deploying TensorFlow models to production environments.

○ **PyTorch ScriptModule:**

- **Description:** PyTorch ScriptModule is a format for serializing PyTorch models using TorchScript, enabling deployment on various platforms.

- **Use Cases:** Deploying PyTorch models to production environments.

3. **API Development:**

○ **REST APIs:**

- **Description:** REST APIs (Representational State Transfer) provide a standardized way to expose model predictions over HTTP. They are widely used for web and mobile applications.

- **Tools:** Flask, FastAPI, Django.

○ **gRPC:**

- **Description:** gRPC (gRPC Remote Procedure Calls) is a high-performance, open-source framework for building APIs. It supports multiple programming languages and provides features like authentication and streaming.

- **Tools:** gRPC libraries for various programming languages.

4. **Model Integration:**
   - **Microservices Architecture:**
     - **Description:** Microservices architecture involves breaking down applications into small, independent services that can be developed, deployed, and scaled independently.
     - **Benefits:** Scalability, flexibility, fault isolation.
   - **Serverless Architecture:**
     - **Description:** Serverless architecture allows developers to build and run applications without managing infrastructure. Models can be deployed as serverless functions that scale automatically based on demand.
     - **Benefits:** Cost-efficiency, automatic scaling, reduced operational overhead.

5. **CI/CD Pipelines:**
   - **Continuous Integration (CI):**
     - **Description:** CI involves automating the process of integrating code changes into a shared repository. It ensures that code changes are tested and validated before merging.
     - **Tools:** Jenkins, GitLab CI, Travis CI.
   - **Continuous Deployment (CD):**
     - **Description:** CD automates the

process of deploying code changes to production environments. It ensures that models are deployed quickly and reliably.

- **Tools:** Kubernetes, Docker, AWS CodePipeline.

Monitoring AI Models

1. **Performance Monitoring:**
   - **Latency:**
     - **Description:** Latency measures the time taken for the model to make predictions. Monitoring latency ensures that the model meets real-time performance requirements.
     - **Tools:** Application performance monitoring tools like Prometheus, Grafana, New Relic.
   - **Throughput:**
     - **Description:** Throughput measures the number of predictions made by the model per unit of time. Monitoring throughput ensures that the model can handle the expected load.
     - **Tools:** Monitoring tools like Prometheus, Grafana, CloudWatch.
   - **Accuracy and Precision:**
     - **Description:** Monitoring the accuracy and precision of the model's predictions ensures that it maintains high performance over time.
     - **Tools:** Custom monitoring scripts, model evaluation metrics.
2. **Drift Detection:**

- **Data Drift:**
  - **Description:** Data drift occurs when the distribution of input data changes over time, leading to degraded model performance.
  - **Techniques:** Statistical tests, monitoring feature distributions, comparing historical and current data.
- **Model Drift:**
  - **Description:** Model drift occurs when the model's performance degrades over time due to changes in data patterns or environmental factors.
  - **Techniques:** Monitoring performance metrics, periodic retraining, model recalibration.

3. **Error Analysis:**
   - **Description:** Error analysis involves identifying and analyzing the errors made by the model to understand their causes and implement corrective measures.
   - **Techniques:** Confusion matrix, error clustering, root cause analysis.

4. **Alerts and Notifications:**
   - **Description:** Setting up alerts and notifications ensures that stakeholders are informed of any performance issues or anomalies in real-time.
   - **Tools:** Monitoring tools like Prometheus, Grafana, CloudWatch, email and messaging services.

Best Practices for AI Deployment and Monitoring

1. **Scalability:**

- Design AI systems to scale horizontally by adding more instances to handle increased load. Use load balancers to distribute traffic evenly.

2. **Fault Tolerance:**

- Implement redundancy and failover mechanisms to ensure that the AI system remains operational in case of failures. Use backup and recovery strategies to handle data loss.

3. **Security:**

- Ensure that the AI system is secure by implementing authentication, authorization, and encryption. Regularly update and patch systems to protect against vulnerabilities.

4. **Versioning:**

- Use version control for models, data, and code to track changes and facilitate rollback if needed. Implement a robust versioning strategy to manage different versions of the model.

5. **Automation:**

- Automate deployment and monitoring processes using CI/CD pipelines and monitoring tools. Automation reduces manual effort and minimizes the risk of errors.

6. **Documentation:**

- Maintain comprehensive documentation for the deployment and monitoring processes, including architecture diagrams, configuration settings, and troubleshooting guides.

7. **Continuous Improvement:**

   ◦ Continuously monitor and evaluate the AI system's performance. Use feedback from monitoring and error analysis to refine and improve the model.

Conclusion

AI deployment and monitoring are essential for ensuring that AI systems operate efficiently, reliably, and securely in production environments. In this chapter, we explored various deployment strategies, model export and serialization techniques, API development, and integration approaches. We also discussed performance monitoring, drift detection, error analysis, and best practices for maintaining AI systems in production.

By following these principles and practices, you can successfully deploy and monitor AI models, ensuring they deliver accurate and timely predictions while maintaining high performance and reliability. As we continue our journey through the subsequent chapters, we will delve deeper into specific aspects of AI implementation and deployment, providing practical insights and guidance.

In the next chapter, we will explore AI in the cloud, discussing the benefits and challenges of cloud-based AI solutions and highlighting major cloud AI providers such as AWS, Google Cloud, and Azure.

CHAPTER 25: AI IN THE CLOUD

Overview

Cloud computing has transformed the way businesses develop, deploy, and scale AI solutions. Cloud-based AI offers numerous advantages, including flexibility, scalability, cost-effectiveness, and access to advanced AI services. This chapter explores the benefits and challenges of cloud-based AI, discusses major cloud AI providers such as AWS, Google Cloud, and Azure, and provides practical insights for leveraging cloud AI services effectively.

Benefits of Cloud-Based AI

1. **Scalability:**
   - Cloud-based AI allows organizations to scale their compute resources up or down based on demand. This ensures that AI models can handle varying workloads without requiring significant upfront investment in hardware.

2. **Cost-Effectiveness:**
   - Cloud AI services operate on a pay-as-you-go model, enabling organizations to pay only for the resources they use. This reduces the need for large capital expenditures on infrastructure.

3. **Flexibility:**
   - Cloud platforms offer a wide range of AI

services and tools, allowing organizations to choose the most suitable solutions for their needs. This includes options for machine learning, deep learning, natural language processing, computer vision, and more.

4. Accessibility:

- Cloud AI services can be accessed from anywhere with an internet connection, making it easy for distributed teams to collaborate on AI projects. This accessibility also supports remote work and global operations.

5. Integration:

- Cloud AI providers offer seamless integration with other cloud services, such as data storage, analytics, and DevOps tools. This simplifies the end-to-end AI workflow and enhances productivity.

6. Maintenance and Updates:

- Cloud AI providers handle infrastructure maintenance, software updates, and security patches, allowing organizations to focus on developing and deploying AI solutions without worrying about underlying infrastructure.

Challenges of Cloud-Based AI

1. Data Privacy and Security:

- Storing and processing data in the cloud raises concerns about data privacy and security. Organizations must ensure that sensitive data is protected and comply with relevant regulations.

2. Latency:

- Real-time applications that require low-latency responses may face challenges with cloud-based AI due to network delays. Edge computing can help mitigate latency issues by processing data closer to the source.

3. **Vendor Lock-In:**

- Relying heavily on a single cloud provider can lead to vendor lock-in, making it difficult to switch providers or migrate to an on-premises solution. Organizations should consider multi-cloud strategies to avoid this risk.

4. **Cost Management:**

- While cloud AI services are cost-effective, organizations must carefully manage their usage to avoid unexpected costs. Monitoring and optimizing resource usage is essential for cost control.

Major Cloud AI Providers

1. **Amazon Web Services (AWS):**

- **Overview:** AWS is a leading cloud provider that offers a comprehensive suite of AI and machine learning services. AWS AI services are designed to cater to a wide range of use cases, from basic AI tasks to advanced machine learning and deep learning applications.

- **Key Services:**

  - **Amazon SageMaker:** A fully managed service for building, training, and deploying machine learning models at scale. SageMaker offers integrated tools for data labeling, model training, hyperparameter tuning, and deployment.

- **Amazon Rekognition:** A computer vision service that enables image and video analysis, including object detection, facial recognition, and scene detection.

- **Amazon Comprehend:** A natural language processing service that provides text analysis, sentiment detection, entity recognition, and language translation.

- **AWS Lambda:** A serverless computing service that allows developers to run code without provisioning or managing servers. It can be used to deploy AI models as serverless functions.

○ **Benefits:**

- Extensive documentation and tutorials.

- Integration with other AWS services, such as S3, DynamoDB, and Redshift.

- Scalability and reliability.

2. **Google Cloud Platform (GCP):**

○ **Overview:** GCP offers a wide range of AI and machine learning services designed to simplify the development and deployment of AI solutions. GCP's AI services leverage Google's expertise in AI research and engineering.

○ **Key Services:**

- **AI Platform:** A suite of tools and services for building, training, and deploying machine learning models. It includes features for data preprocessing, model training, hyperparameter tuning, and model management.

- **Vision AI:** A computer vision service that provides image and video analysis, including object detection, face detection, and OCR.
- **Natural Language AI:** A natural language processing service that offers text analysis, sentiment detection, entity recognition, and language translation.
- **BigQuery ML:** A service that allows users to build and deploy machine learning models directly within BigQuery using SQL.

- **Benefits:**
  - Powerful data analytics and processing capabilities.
  - Integration with Google services, such as Google Drive, Google Sheets, and Google Analytics.
  - Strong support for open-source frameworks and tools.

3. **Microsoft Azure:**
  - **Overview:** Azure provides a comprehensive set of AI and machine learning services designed to support a wide range of use cases. Azure AI services are integrated with the broader Azure ecosystem, making it easy to build and deploy AI solutions.
  - **Key Services:**
    - **Azure Machine Learning:** A fully

managed service for building, training, and deploying machine learning models. It offers tools for data preprocessing, model training, hyperparameter tuning, and model management.

- **Azure Cognitive Services:** A collection of APIs and services for computer vision, natural language processing, speech recognition, and decision-making.
- **Azure Bot Service:** A platform for building, testing, and deploying conversational agents and chatbots.
- **Azure Functions:** A serverless computing service that allows developers to run code without provisioning or managing servers. It can be used to deploy AI models as serverless functions.

○ **Benefits:**

- Integration with other Microsoft products and services, such as Office 365, Dynamics 365, and Power BI.
- Strong support for enterprise-grade security and compliance.
- Flexible pricing and cost management options.

Practical Insights for Leveraging Cloud AI Services

1. **Choosing the Right Provider:**
   ○ Evaluate the specific needs of your AI project and compare the offerings of different cloud providers. Consider factors such as available services, integration capabilities, pricing, and

support.

2. **Data Management:**

   - Ensure that data is stored securely and complies with relevant regulations. Use cloud-native data storage solutions, such as AWS S3, Google Cloud Storage, and Azure Blob Storage, for scalable and reliable data management.

3. **Security Best Practices:**

   - Implement robust security measures, such as encryption, access control, and regular security audits. Use cloud provider tools and services for security monitoring and threat detection.

4. **Cost Optimization:**

   - Monitor and optimize resource usage to control costs. Use cloud provider tools, such as AWS Cost Explorer, Google Cloud Billing, and Azure Cost Management, to track expenses and identify cost-saving opportunities.

5. **Scalability and Performance:**

   - Design AI solutions to scale horizontally and handle varying workloads. Use cloud-native services, such as load balancers and auto-scaling, to ensure high performance and reliability.

6. **Continuous Monitoring and Maintenance:**

   - Continuously monitor the performance of deployed AI models and infrastructure. Use cloud provider monitoring tools, such as Amazon CloudWatch, Google Cloud Monitoring, and Azure Monitor, to track key metrics and set up alerts.

Conclusion

Cloud-based AI offers numerous advantages, including scalability, cost-effectiveness, flexibility, and access to advanced AI services. In this chapter, we explored the benefits and challenges of cloud-based AI, discussed major cloud AI providers such as AWS, Google Cloud, and Azure, and provided practical insights for leveraging cloud AI services effectively.

By understanding the strengths and offerings of different cloud providers and implementing best practices for cloud AI deployment and management, organizations can harness the power of cloud AI to drive innovation and achieve their business goals. As we continue our journey through the subsequent chapters, we will delve deeper into specific aspects of AI implementation and deployment, providing practical insights and guidance.

In the next chapter, we will explore ethical considerations in AI, discussing the importance of fairness, transparency, and accountability in AI systems and highlighting strategies for addressing ethical challenges.

CHAPTER 26: ETHICAL CONSIDERATIONS IN AI

Overview

As artificial intelligence (AI) continues to advance and permeate various aspects of society, it is crucial to address the ethical considerations associated with its development and deployment. Ethical AI ensures that AI systems are fair, transparent, accountable, and respect the rights and dignity of individuals. This chapter explores the importance of ethical considerations in AI, key ethical principles, common ethical challenges, and strategies for promoting ethical AI practices.

Importance of Ethical Considerations in AI

1. **Fairness:**
    - Ensuring that AI systems do not discriminate against individuals or groups based on attributes such as race, gender, age, or socioeconomic status. Fairness in AI promotes equality and social justice.

2. **Transparency:**
    - Providing clear and understandable explanations for AI decisions and processes. Transparency builds trust and allows stakeholders to evaluate the reliability and integrity of AI systems.

3. Accountability:

- Establishing mechanisms to hold developers, organizations, and AI systems accountable for their actions and decisions. Accountability ensures that ethical standards are upheld and that any negative impacts are addressed.

4. Privacy:

- Protecting individuals' data privacy and ensuring that AI systems comply with data protection regulations. Privacy is essential for maintaining trust and safeguarding personal information.

5. Safety:

- Ensuring that AI systems operate safely and do not cause harm to individuals or society. Safety considerations include minimizing risks, preventing misuse, and addressing unintended consequences.

6. Inclusivity:

- Promoting the inclusion of diverse perspectives and experiences in AI development. Inclusivity ensures that AI systems are designed to serve and benefit all members of society.

Key Ethical Principles in AI

1. Fairness and Non-Discrimination:

- AI systems should treat all individuals and groups equitably, without bias or discrimination. This includes addressing both direct and indirect biases in data and algorithms.

2. Transparency and Explainability:

- AI systems should provide clear and

understandable explanations for their decisions and processes. Stakeholders should be able to understand how AI models work and why certain decisions are made.

3. **Accountability and Responsibility:**
   ◦ Developers and organizations should be accountable for the ethical implications of their AI systems. This includes establishing clear lines of responsibility and implementing mechanisms for redress in case of harm.

4. **Privacy and Data Protection:**
   ◦ AI systems should respect individuals' privacy and comply with data protection regulations. Data should be collected, stored, and processed in a manner that protects personal information and minimizes privacy risks.

5. **Safety and Security:**
   ◦ AI systems should be designed and deployed with safety and security in mind. This includes ensuring that AI systems do not cause harm, preventing misuse, and addressing vulnerabilities.

6. **Inclusivity and Diversity:**
   ◦ AI development should involve diverse perspectives and experiences to ensure that AI systems are inclusive and serve the needs of all members of society. This includes considering the impact of AI on marginalized and underrepresented groups.

Common Ethical Challenges in AI

1. **Bias and Discrimination:**
   ◦ AI systems can inadvertently perpetuate and amplify biases present in training data. This

can lead to discriminatory outcomes, such as biased hiring practices or unfair credit scoring.

○ **Strategies:**

  ▪ Conduct bias audits and impact assessments to identify and mitigate biases in data and algorithms.

  ▪ Use diverse and representative datasets for training AI models.

  ▪ Implement fairness-enhancing techniques, such as reweighting, adversarial debiasing, and fairness constraints.

2. **Lack of Transparency and Explainability:**

○ Complex AI models, such as deep learning networks, can be challenging to interpret and understand. This lack of transparency can undermine trust and accountability.

○ **Strategies:**

  ▪ Use model-agnostic interpretation techniques, such as LIME (Local Interpretable Model-agnostic Explanations) and SHAP (SHapley Additive exPlanations).

  ▪ Develop inherently interpretable models, such as decision trees and linear models, where possible.

  ▪ Provide clear and user-friendly explanations for AI decisions.

3. **Data Privacy and Security:**

○ AI systems often require large amounts of data, raising concerns about data privacy and security. Unauthorized access or misuse of data can lead to privacy breaches and harm.

- **Strategies:**
  - Implement robust data protection measures, such as encryption, access control, and anonymization.
  - Comply with data protection regulations, such as GDPR (General Data Protection Regulation) and CCPA (California Consumer Privacy Act).
  - Conduct regular security audits and risk assessments to identify and address vulnerabilities.

4. **Autonomous Decision-Making:**
   - Autonomous AI systems, such as self-driving cars and autonomous drones, make decisions without human intervention. Ensuring the safety and reliability of these systems is critical.
   - **Strategies:**
     - Conduct rigorous testing and validation of autonomous systems in diverse scenarios.
     - Implement fail-safe mechanisms and redundancy to ensure safety.
     - Establish clear guidelines and regulations for the deployment and use of autonomous AI systems.

5. **Ethical Use and Misuse:**
   - AI systems can be used for unethical purposes, such as surveillance, deepfakes, and autonomous weapons. Addressing the potential for misuse is essential for ethical AI.
   - **Strategies:**

- Establish ethical guidelines and codes of conduct for AI development and use.
- Implement mechanisms for monitoring and preventing the misuse of AI technologies.
- Promote public awareness and education about the ethical implications of AI.

Strategies for Promoting Ethical AI Practices

1. **Ethical Frameworks and Guidelines:**
   - Develop and adopt ethical frameworks and guidelines for AI development and deployment. These frameworks should outline ethical principles, best practices, and standards for responsible AI.
   - **Examples:**
     - The IEEE Global Initiative on Ethics of Autonomous and Intelligent Systems provides a comprehensive framework for ethical AI.
     - The European Commission's Ethics Guidelines for Trustworthy AI outline principles for ensuring AI is lawful, ethical, and robust.

2. **Bias Audits and Impact Assessments:**
   - Conduct regular bias audits and impact assessments to identify and address ethical concerns in AI systems. These assessments should evaluate the potential impact of AI on different stakeholders and identify areas for improvement.

3. **Ethics Committees and Review Boards:**

- Establish ethics committees and review boards to oversee AI projects and ensure compliance with ethical guidelines. These committees should include diverse stakeholders, such as ethicists, legal experts, and representatives from affected communities.

4. **Inclusive and Diverse Teams:**

- Promote diversity and inclusion in AI development teams to ensure that AI systems are designed to serve the needs of all members of society. Diverse teams bring different perspectives and experiences, which can help identify and address ethical concerns.

5. **Transparency and Communication:**

- Communicate transparently with stakeholders about the development, deployment, and impact of AI systems. Provide clear and accessible information about AI decisions and processes to build trust and accountability.

6. **Continuous Monitoring and Evaluation:**

- Continuously monitor and evaluate the performance and ethical implications of AI systems. Implement mechanisms for feedback and redress to address any negative impacts and improve the system over time.

Conclusion

Ethical considerations are crucial for the responsible development and deployment of AI systems. Ensuring that AI is fair, transparent, accountable, and respectful of privacy and safety is essential for building trust and promoting positive societal impact. In this chapter, we explored the importance of ethical considerations in AI, key ethical principles, common ethical challenges, and strategies for promoting ethical AI practices.

By adhering to ethical principles and implementing best practices, organizations can develop AI systems that are not only effective but also aligned with societal values and expectations. As we continue our journey through the subsequent chapters, we will delve deeper into specific aspects of AI implementation and deployment, providing practical insights and guidance.

In the next chapter, we will explore the future of AI, discussing emerging trends, potential breakthroughs, and the impact of AI on various industries and society as a whole.

CHAPTER 27: THE FUTURE OF AI

Overview

Artificial Intelligence (AI) is poised to transform various aspects of society and industry, bringing about significant advancements and challenges. As we look to the future, it is essential to understand the emerging trends, potential breakthroughs, and the broader impact of AI on different domains. This chapter explores the future of AI, discussing the advancements in AI technologies, their applications, ethical considerations, and the potential societal changes driven by AI.

Emerging Trends in AI

1. **Explainable AI (XAI):**
   - **Description:** The demand for transparency and interpretability in AI systems is driving the development of explainable AI techniques. XAI aims to provide clear and understandable explanations for AI decisions, enhancing trust and accountability.
   - **Impact:** Increased adoption of XAI will lead to more transparent AI systems, improved regulatory compliance, and greater trust among users and stakeholders.

2. **AI-Driven Automation:**
   - **Description:** AI is automating various tasks across industries, from manufacturing and logistics to customer service and healthcare.

Automation powered by AI is increasing efficiency, reducing costs, and transforming business processes.

- **Impact:** Widespread AI-driven automation will lead to significant productivity gains, reshaping job markets, and requiring workforce reskilling and upskilling.

3. **AI in Healthcare:**

- **Description:** AI is revolutionizing healthcare by enabling early disease detection, personalized treatment plans, and improved patient outcomes. AI-driven diagnostics, predictive analytics, and robotic surgeries are becoming increasingly prevalent.

- **Impact:** AI in healthcare will lead to more accurate diagnoses, better patient care, and reduced healthcare costs. However, ethical considerations related to data privacy and bias must be addressed.

4. **Edge AI:**

- **Description:** Edge AI involves deploying AI models on edge devices, such as smartphones, IoT devices, and autonomous vehicles. This approach reduces latency and enables real-time decision-making without relying on cloud infrastructure.

- **Impact:** Edge AI will enhance the performance and responsiveness of AI applications, particularly in areas like autonomous driving, smart cities, and industrial automation.

5. **AI and Quantum Computing:**

- **Description:** Quantum computing has the potential to solve complex problems that are currently intractable for classical computers. Integrating AI with quantum computing can accelerate advancements in fields such as cryptography, material science, and optimization.

- **Impact:** The combination of AI and quantum computing will lead to breakthroughs in scientific research, secure communications, and advanced AI algorithms.

6. **AI for Climate Change:**

- **Description:** AI is being used to address climate change by optimizing energy consumption, predicting environmental changes, and supporting sustainable practices. AI-driven models are helping researchers understand and mitigate the impact of climate change.

- **Impact:** AI will play a crucial role in promoting sustainability, reducing carbon footprints, and developing innovative solutions to combat climate change.

Potential Breakthroughs in AI

1. **Artificial General Intelligence (AGI):**

- **Description:** AGI refers to AI systems that possess the ability to understand, learn, and apply knowledge across a wide range of tasks, similar to human intelligence. Achieving AGI remains a long-term goal in AI research.

- **Impact:** AGI could revolutionize numerous fields, from scientific discovery to creative arts, leading to unprecedented advancements and raising important ethical and philosophical questions.

2. **Neuromorphic Computing:**

- **Description:** Neuromorphic computing involves designing hardware that mimics the structure and function of the human brain. This approach aims to create energy-efficient AI systems capable of processing information in a manner similar to biological neurons.
- **Impact:** Neuromorphic computing could lead to significant advancements in AI, enabling more efficient and adaptive systems with enhanced cognitive capabilities.

3. **Federated Learning:**

- **Description:** Federated learning enables AI models to be trained across decentralized devices without sharing raw data. This approach enhances data privacy and security while leveraging the collective intelligence of distributed networks.
- **Impact:** Federated learning will promote collaborative AI development, protect user privacy, and enable AI applications in sensitive domains such as healthcare and finance.

4. **AI-Enhanced Creativity:**

- **Description:** AI is increasingly being used to augment human creativity, generating art, music, literature, and design. AI-powered creative tools are assisting artists, writers, and designers in exploring new possibilities and pushing the boundaries of creativity.
- **Impact:** AI-enhanced creativity will lead to new forms of artistic expression, innovative design solutions, and collaborative human-AI creative processes.

5. **Human-AI Collaboration:**

- **Description:** The future of AI involves seamless collaboration between humans and AI systems, leveraging the strengths of both to solve complex problems. AI will act as an augmentative tool, enhancing human decision-making and productivity.
- **Impact:** Human-AI collaboration will lead to more effective problem-solving, improved decision-making, and enhanced productivity across various domains.

Ethical Considerations for Future AI

1. Bias and Fairness:

- **Challenge:** Ensuring that AI systems are free from bias and treat all individuals and groups equitably.
- **Strategies:** Implementing fairness-enhancing techniques, conducting bias audits, and using diverse and representative datasets.

2. Transparency and Accountability:

- **Challenge:** Providing clear explanations for AI decisions and establishing accountability for AI actions.
- **Strategies:** Developing explainable AI techniques, implementing regulatory frameworks, and establishing ethics committees.

3. Data Privacy and Security:

- **Challenge:** Protecting individuals' data privacy and ensuring secure data processing.
- **Strategies:** Implementing robust data protection measures, complying with data protection regulations, and promoting privacy-preserving techniques.

4. **Safety and Reliability:**
    - **Challenge:** Ensuring that AI systems operate safely and do not cause harm.
    - **Strategies:** Conducting rigorous testing and validation, implementing fail-safe mechanisms, and establishing safety standards.

5. **Ethical Use and Misuse:**
    - **Challenge:** Preventing the misuse of AI technologies and promoting ethical use.
    - **Strategies:** Establishing ethical guidelines, monitoring AI applications, and promoting public awareness and education.

Impact of AI on Industries and Society

1. **Healthcare:**
    - **Impact:** AI will enhance diagnostics, personalized medicine, and patient care, leading to improved health outcomes and reduced healthcare costs.

2. **Finance:**
    - **Impact:** AI will transform financial services, enabling more accurate risk assessment, fraud detection, and personalized financial advice.

3. **Manufacturing:**
    - **Impact:** AI-driven automation will increase efficiency, reduce production costs, and enable predictive maintenance in manufacturing processes.

4. **Retail:**
    - **Impact:** AI will enhance customer experiences through personalized recommendations, inventory management,

and automated customer service.

5. **Education:**

   ◦ **Impact:** AI-powered educational tools will provide personalized learning experiences, adaptive assessments, and support for diverse learning needs.

6. **Transportation:**

   ◦ **Impact:** Autonomous vehicles and AI-driven logistics will improve transportation efficiency, reduce accidents, and transform supply chains.

7. **Entertainment:**

   ◦ **Impact:** AI will revolutionize content creation, recommendation systems, and immersive experiences in the entertainment industry.

Conclusion

The future of AI holds immense potential for transforming industries and society, driving innovation, and addressing global challenges. Emerging trends such as explainable AI, AI-driven automation, edge AI, and AI for climate change are shaping the next generation of AI technologies. Potential breakthroughs in AGI, neuromorphic computing, federated learning, and AI-enhanced creativity will push the boundaries of what AI can achieve.

However, as AI continues to evolve, it is essential to address ethical considerations and ensure that AI systems are developed and deployed responsibly. By promoting fairness, transparency, accountability, and inclusivity, we can harness the power of AI to create a positive and equitable future for all.

As we conclude this book, we hope that the insights and knowledge shared have provided you with a comprehensive understanding of AI, its applications, and the considerations for building and deploying AI systems. The journey of AI is ongoing, and we encourage you to stay curious, continue learning, and contribute to the responsible advancement of artificial intelligence.

CHAPTER 28: AI
IN EDUCATION

Overview

AI is transforming the education sector by enabling personalized learning, automating administrative tasks, and enhancing teaching methods. The integration of AI in education aims to improve learning outcomes, increase access to education, and support educators in delivering effective instruction. This chapter explores the impact of AI on education, key applications, challenges, and future trends.

Impact of AI on Education

1. **Personalized Learning:**
   - AI enables personalized learning experiences tailored to individual students' needs, preferences, and learning styles. By analyzing student data, AI can recommend customized learning paths, resources, and activities.
   - **Benefits:** Improved student engagement, better learning outcomes, and enhanced motivation.

2. **Adaptive Learning Technologies:**
   - Adaptive learning technologies use AI to dynamically adjust the difficulty and content of educational materials based on student performance and progress. These systems provide real-time feedback and support to help students master concepts.

- **Benefits:** Increased learning efficiency, targeted support for struggling students, and accelerated progression for advanced learners.

3. **Intelligent Tutoring Systems:**

   - Intelligent tutoring systems (ITS) use AI to provide one-on-one tutoring to students. These systems can diagnose learning gaps, offer explanations, and guide students through problem-solving processes.
   - **Benefits:** Personalized instruction, increased accessibility to high-quality tutoring, and improved mastery of subjects.

4. **Automated Grading and Assessment:**

   - AI-powered tools can automatically grade assignments, quizzes, and exams, providing instant feedback to students. These tools can also analyze student performance to identify areas for improvement.
   - **Benefits:** Reduced workload for educators, timely feedback for students, and data-driven insights into student performance.

5. **Natural Language Processing (NLP) for Education:**

   - NLP technologies enable AI to understand and generate human language, supporting applications such as automated essay scoring, language translation, and conversational agents.
   - **Benefits:** Enhanced language learning, support for multilingual education, and improved communication between students and educators.

6. **AI-Enhanced Learning Analytics:**

- Learning analytics use AI to analyze data from various educational activities to gain insights into student behavior, engagement, and performance. These insights can inform instructional strategies and interventions.
- **Benefits:** Data-driven decision-making, early identification of at-risk students, and improved instructional planning.

Key Applications of AI in Education

1. **Personalized Learning Platforms:**
   - **Description:** AI-driven platforms that provide personalized learning experiences by recommending content, activities, and assessments based on individual student data.
   - **Examples:** Knewton, DreamBox, Smart Sparrow.

2. **Intelligent Tutoring Systems:**
   - **Description:** AI-powered systems that offer personalized tutoring and guidance to students, mimicking the role of a human tutor.
   - **Examples:** Carnegie Learning, ALEKS, Squirrel AI.

3. **Automated Grading Tools:**
   - **Description:** Tools that use AI to automatically grade assignments, quizzes, and exams, providing instant feedback to students.
   - **Examples:** Gradescope, Turnitin, LightSide.

4. **Conversational Agents and Chatbots:**
   - **Description:** AI-powered conversational agents that can answer student queries,

provide explanations, and offer support for various educational tasks.

- **Examples:** IBM Watson Tutor, Duolingo Chatbots, Ada.

5. **Language Learning Applications:**

- **Description:** AI-driven applications that support language learning through personalized lessons, speech recognition, and real-time feedback.

- **Examples:** Duolingo, Babbel, Rosetta Stone.

6. **Learning Management Systems (LMS) with AI:**

- **Description:** LMS platforms that integrate AI to provide personalized learning experiences, track student progress, and recommend resources.

- **Examples:** Moodle with AI plugins, Canvas with AI integration, Blackboard with AI capabilities.

Challenges of AI in Education

1. **Data Privacy and Security:**

- **Challenge:** Ensuring that student data is protected and used responsibly, complying with data protection regulations such as FERPA (Family Educational Rights and Privacy Act) and GDPR.

- **Strategies:** Implement robust data protection measures, obtain informed consent, and ensure transparency in data usage.

2. **Bias and Fairness:**

- **Challenge:** Addressing biases in AI algorithms that may lead to unfair treatment of certain students or groups.

- **Strategies:** Use diverse and representative

datasets, conduct bias audits, and implement fairness-enhancing techniques.

3. **Accessibility and Inclusivity:**
   - **Challenge:** Ensuring that AI-driven educational tools are accessible to all students, including those with disabilities and from diverse backgrounds.
   - **Strategies:** Design inclusive and accessible interfaces, provide multilingual support, and consider the needs of marginalized groups.

4. **Educator Training and Support:**
   - **Challenge:** Providing educators with the necessary training and support to effectively integrate AI technologies into their teaching practices.
   - **Strategies:** Offer professional development programs, create resources and guides, and foster a culture of continuous learning.

5. **Cost and Resource Allocation:**
   - **Challenge:** Managing the costs associated with implementing and maintaining AI-driven educational technologies.
   - **Strategies:** Seek funding and grants, collaborate with edtech companies, and prioritize investments based on educational impact.

Future Trends in AI in Education

1. **Enhanced Personalization:**
   - AI will continue to advance in providing highly personalized learning experiences, leveraging more sophisticated algorithms and data insights to tailor instruction to individual student needs.

2. **AI-Driven Content Creation:**

   ◦ AI will play a greater role in creating and curating educational content, generating interactive and engaging materials that adapt to student preferences and learning styles.

3. **Virtual and Augmented Reality:**

   ◦ The integration of AI with virtual and augmented reality will create immersive learning experiences, enabling students to explore complex concepts and environments in a hands-on manner.

4. **Lifelong Learning and Upskilling:**

   ◦ AI-driven platforms will support lifelong learning and upskilling, providing personalized recommendations for continuous education and professional development.

5. **AI for Teacher Support:**

   ◦ AI will increasingly assist educators in administrative tasks, instructional planning, and professional development, allowing them to focus more on teaching and mentoring.

6. **Global Collaboration and Access:**

   ◦ AI will facilitate global collaboration and access to quality education, connecting students and educators from different regions and fostering a more inclusive and diverse learning community.

Conclusion

AI is revolutionizing education by enabling personalized learning, enhancing teaching methods, and improving administrative efficiency. The integration of AI in education holds immense potential for improving learning outcomes and increasing access to quality education. However, it also presents challenges related to data privacy, bias, accessibility, and cost. By addressing these challenges and leveraging the opportunities offered by AI, educators and policymakers can create a more equitable and effective education system.

As we look to the future, the continued advancement of AI technologies will further transform education, creating new possibilities for personalized and immersive learning experiences. By embracing AI responsibly and ethically, we can ensure that the benefits of AI in education are realized for all learners.

CHAPTER 29: AI IN FINANCE

Overview

The finance industry has been significantly transformed by the integration of artificial intelligence (AI). AI technologies are enhancing various aspects of finance, from automating routine tasks to providing deeper insights and making informed decisions. This chapter delves into the impact of AI on the finance sector, key applications, challenges, and future trends.

Impact of AI on Finance

1. **Automated Trading:**
    - AI-driven algorithms are revolutionizing trading by making real-time decisions based on vast amounts of data. These algorithms can analyze market conditions, identify patterns, and execute trades at high speeds, often outperforming human traders.
    - **Benefits:** Increased trading efficiency, reduced latency, improved accuracy, and the ability to operate continuously without fatigue.

2. **Risk Management:**
    - AI is enhancing risk management by providing advanced analytics and predictive modeling. AI systems can identify potential risks, assess their impact, and recommend mitigation strategies. This is particularly valuable for credit risk assessment, fraud

detection, and market risk analysis.

- **Benefits:** Improved risk assessment accuracy, early detection of potential issues, and better-informed decision-making.

3. **Personalized Financial Services:**

- AI enables financial institutions to offer personalized services to their customers. By analyzing customer data and behavior, AI systems can recommend tailored financial products, provide personalized advice, and enhance customer experiences.

- **Benefits:** Increased customer satisfaction, higher engagement, and more effective cross-selling and up-selling opportunities.

4. **Fraud Detection and Prevention:**

- AI-powered systems are highly effective at detecting and preventing fraudulent activities. By analyzing transaction patterns and identifying anomalies, AI can detect suspicious behavior in real-time and alert financial institutions.

- **Benefits:** Reduced fraud losses, improved security, and enhanced customer trust.

5. **Financial Forecasting:**

- AI technologies, such as machine learning and natural language processing, are being used to improve financial forecasting. These systems can analyze historical data, market trends, and external factors to make accurate predictions about future financial performance.

- **Benefits:** Better investment decisions, improved financial planning, and enhanced strategic planning.

Key Applications of AI in Finance

1. Algorithmic Trading:

- **Description:** Using AI-driven algorithms to execute trades automatically based on predefined strategies and real-time market data.
- **Examples:** High-frequency trading, quantitative trading, and arbitrage strategies.

2. Credit Scoring:

- **Description:** AI-powered models assess the creditworthiness of individuals and businesses by analyzing various data points, including credit history, financial behavior, and social media activity.
- **Examples:** FICO Score, Zest AI, Lenddo.

3. Robo-Advisors:

- **Description:** AI-driven platforms that provide automated, algorithm-based financial planning and investment advice without human intervention.
- **Examples:** Betterment, Wealthfront, Robinhood.

4. Customer Service Chatbots:

- **Description:** AI-powered chatbots assist customers with banking inquiries, transactions, and account management through natural language processing and machine learning.
- **Examples:** Erica by Bank of America, Eno by Capital One, Amex Bot by American Express.

5. Anti-Money Laundering (AML):

- **Description:** AI systems detect and prevent money laundering activities by analyzing transaction data and identifying suspicious patterns and behaviors.

- **Examples:** NICE Actimize, ComplyAdvantage, Palantir.

6. **Portfolio Management:**

- **Description:** AI-powered tools assist portfolio managers in optimizing asset allocation, rebalancing portfolios, and managing risk based on real-time data and predictive analytics.
- **Examples:** BlackRock's Aladdin, SigFig, Charles Schwab's Intelligent Portfolios.

Challenges of AI in Finance

1. **Data Privacy and Security:**

- **Challenge:** Ensuring that sensitive financial data is protected and used responsibly, complying with data protection regulations such as GDPR and CCPA.
- **Strategies:** Implement robust data protection measures, encrypt data, and ensure compliance with regulations.

2. **Bias and Fairness:**

- **Challenge:** Addressing biases in AI algorithms that may lead to unfair treatment of certain individuals or groups, particularly in areas like credit scoring and lending.
- **Strategies:** Use diverse and representative datasets, conduct bias audits, and implement fairness-enhancing techniques.

3. **Regulatory Compliance:**

- **Challenge:** Ensuring that AI systems comply with complex and evolving financial regulations, such as those related to anti-money laundering, fraud prevention, and consumer protection.

- **Strategies:** Stay informed about regulatory changes, collaborate with legal experts, and implement compliance monitoring systems.

4. **Transparency and Explainability:**

- **Challenge:** Providing clear and understandable explanations for AI-driven financial decisions, which is critical for building trust with customers and regulators.
- **Strategies:** Use explainable AI techniques, provide detailed documentation, and ensure transparency in AI processes.

5. **Integration with Legacy Systems:**

- **Challenge:** Integrating AI technologies with existing legacy systems in financial institutions can be complex and costly.
- **Strategies:** Develop integration plans, use middleware solutions, and prioritize systems modernization.

Future Trends in AI in Finance

1. **Hybrid Human-AI Decision-Making:**

- Combining human expertise with AI-driven insights will become more prevalent, enhancing decision-making processes in finance. AI will assist humans in analyzing data, identifying trends, and making informed decisions.

2. **Advanced Fraud Detection:**

- AI will continue to evolve in detecting and preventing fraud, leveraging advanced techniques such as deep learning and anomaly detection. Real-time monitoring and predictive analytics will enhance security measures.

3. **RegTech Solutions:**

   ◦ Regulatory technology (RegTech) solutions powered by AI will streamline compliance processes, reduce regulatory burdens, and improve risk management. AI will help automate reporting, monitoring, and regulatory compliance.

4. **AI-Driven Financial Wellness:**

   ◦ AI-powered tools will support individuals in managing their finances, improving financial literacy, and achieving financial wellness. Personalized recommendations and automated budgeting will enhance financial planning.

5. **Blockchain and AI Integration:**

   ◦ The integration of AI with blockchain technology will enhance transparency, security, and efficiency in financial transactions. AI will analyze blockchain data to detect fraud, predict trends, and optimize processes.

6. **Enhanced Customer Experiences:**

   ◦ AI will continue to improve customer experiences in finance by providing personalized services, seamless interactions, and proactive support. AI-driven insights will help financial institutions anticipate customer needs and preferences.

Conclusion

AI is revolutionizing the finance industry by enhancing trading, risk management, personalized services, fraud detection, and financial forecasting. The integration of AI in finance holds immense potential for improving efficiency, accuracy, and customer experiences. However, it also presents challenges related to data privacy, bias, regulatory compliance, transparency, and integration with legacy systems. By addressing these challenges and leveraging AI technologies, financial institutions can unlock new opportunities and drive innovation in the sector.

As we look to the future, the continued advancement of AI in finance will further transform the industry, creating new possibilities for hybrid decision-making, advanced fraud detection, RegTech solutions, financial wellness, and enhanced customer experiences. By embracing AI responsibly and ethically, we can ensure that the benefits of AI in finance are realized for all stakeholders.

CHAPTER 30: AI IN ENTERTAINMENT

Overview

The entertainment industry is experiencing a profound transformation through the integration of artificial intelligence (AI). From content creation and recommendation systems to interactive experiences and virtual reality, AI is enhancing the way we create, consume, and engage with entertainment. This chapter explores the impact of AI on the entertainment sector, key applications, challenges, and future trends.

Impact of AI on Entertainment

1. **Content Creation:**
   - AI is revolutionizing content creation by assisting writers, musicians, and artists in generating new and innovative works. AI-powered tools can create music, write scripts, generate visual art, and even produce entire films.
   - **Benefits:** Increased creativity, faster production times, and the ability to explore new artistic possibilities.

2. **Recommendation Systems:**
   - AI-driven recommendation systems are improving the way we discover and consume entertainment content. By analyzing user behavior and preferences, these systems can recommend personalized content, such as

movies, music, books, and games.

- **Benefits:** Enhanced user experience, increased engagement, and more relevant content discovery.

3. **Interactive Experiences:**

- AI is enabling the development of interactive and immersive entertainment experiences. Virtual reality (VR), augmented reality (AR), and interactive storytelling are creating new ways for audiences to engage with content.
- **Benefits:** Immersive experiences, increased interactivity, and greater audience participation.

4. **Gaming:**

- AI is transforming the gaming industry by creating more realistic and intelligent non-player characters (NPCs), procedural content generation, and adaptive gameplay. AI can also be used to create realistic graphics and simulate complex physics.
- **Benefits:** Enhanced gameplay experiences, improved graphics, and more dynamic game worlds.

5. **Video Editing and Post-Production:**

- AI-powered tools are streamlining video editing and post-production processes. These tools can automate tasks such as color correction, scene detection, and visual effects, making the editing process more efficient.
- **Benefits:** Faster post-production, reduced costs, and higher-quality video content.

6. **Audience Analytics:**

- AI is helping entertainment companies

gain insights into audience behavior and preferences. By analyzing data from various sources, AI can provide valuable insights into audience demographics, engagement, and sentiment.

◦ **Benefits:** Data-driven decision-making, better content targeting, and improved audience engagement.

Key Applications of AI in Entertainment

1. **AI-Generated Music:**

   ◦ **Description:** AI algorithms can compose music in various genres and styles, assisting musicians in creating new compositions and soundtracks.

   ◦ **Examples:** OpenAI's MuseNet, Amper Music, AIVA (Artificial Intelligence Virtual Artist).

2. **Script and Story Writing:**

   ◦ **Description:** AI-powered tools can assist writers in generating story ideas, writing scripts, and creating dialogue. These tools can analyze existing literature and generate new content based on patterns and styles.

   ◦ **Examples:** OpenAI's GPT-3, ScriptBook, Plotagon.

3. **Visual Art and Animation:**

   ◦ **Description:** AI can create visual art, generate animations, and assist artists in the creative process. AI-powered tools can produce realistic images, generate art in specific styles, and automate animation tasks.

   ◦ **Examples:** DeepArt, RunwayML, Artbreeder.

4. **Content Recommendation:**

   ◦ **Description:** AI-driven recommendation

systems analyze user behavior and preferences to suggest personalized content, such as movies, TV shows, music, and books.

- **Examples:** Netflix's recommendation algorithm, Spotify's Discover Weekly, Amazon's book recommendations.

5. **Virtual and Augmented Reality:**

- **Description:** AI enhances VR and AR experiences by creating realistic environments, intelligent characters, and interactive storytelling. AI can also be used to generate virtual worlds and simulate real-life scenarios.
- **Examples:** Oculus VR, Google ARCore, Niantic's Pokémon GO.

6. **Interactive Storytelling:**

- **Description:** AI-powered interactive storytelling allows audiences to influence the narrative and outcome of stories. These experiences can adapt to user choices and create personalized storylines.
- **Examples:** Netflix's Black Mirror: Bandersnatch, AI Dungeon, The Walking Dead: Our World.

Challenges of AI in Entertainment

1. **Creativity and Originality:**

- **Challenge:** Ensuring that AI-generated content is original and creative, rather than derivative or formulaic.
- **Strategies:** Use AI as a tool to augment human creativity, collaborate with artists, and continuously refine AI algorithms.

2. **Intellectual Property:**

○ **Challenge:** Addressing intellectual property (IP) concerns related to AI-generated content, including ownership and copyright issues.

○ **Strategies:** Establish clear guidelines for IP rights, collaborate with legal experts, and develop fair licensing agreements.

3. **Ethical Considerations:**

○ **Challenge:** Ensuring that AI-generated content is ethical and does not perpetuate harmful stereotypes or biases.

○ **Strategies:** Conduct bias audits, implement fairness-enhancing techniques, and involve diverse perspectives in the creative process.

4. **Audience Acceptance:**

○ **Challenge:** Gaining audience acceptance and trust in AI-generated content and experiences.

○ **Strategies:** Educate audiences about AI, emphasize the collaborative nature of AI and human creativity, and focus on delivering high-quality content.

5. **Data Privacy:**

○ **Challenge:** Protecting user data and ensuring that recommendation systems and analytics respect privacy regulations.

○ **Strategies:** Implement robust data protection measures, obtain informed consent, and comply with data protection regulations.

Future Trends in AI in Entertainment

1. **Enhanced AI-Creativity Collaboration:**

○ The future of AI in entertainment will see increased collaboration between AI and human creators. AI will serve as a tool to inspire and enhance human creativity, leading to innovative and diverse content.

2. **AI-Driven Personalization:**

   ◦ AI will continue to refine personalization algorithms, providing even more tailored recommendations and experiences to individual users. This will enhance user engagement and satisfaction.

3. **Immersive Experiences:**

   ◦ AI will play a crucial role in creating more immersive and interactive entertainment experiences. Advances in VR, AR, and mixed reality will provide audiences with new ways to engage with content.

4. **Real-Time Content Generation:**

   ◦ AI will enable real-time content generation, allowing for dynamic and responsive entertainment experiences. This includes live performances, interactive games, and adaptive storytelling.

5. **Integration with Blockchain:**

   ◦ The integration of AI with blockchain technology will enhance transparency, security, and provenance in the entertainment industry. This will support fair compensation for creators and protect intellectual property.

6. **AI-Empowered Fan Engagement:**

   ◦ AI will enhance fan engagement by providing personalized interactions, social media insights, and real-time feedback. This will create stronger connections between creators and their audiences.

Conclusion

AI is transforming the entertainment industry by enhancing content creation, improving recommendation systems, and enabling interactive experiences. The integration of AI in entertainment holds immense potential for increasing creativity, efficiency, and audience engagement. However, it also presents challenges related to creativity, intellectual property, ethics, audience acceptance, and data privacy. By addressing these challenges and leveraging AI technologies, the entertainment industry can unlock new opportunities and drive innovation.

As we look to the future, the continued advancement of AI in entertainment will further transform the industry, creating new possibilities for AI-human collaboration, personalization, immersive experiences, real-time content generation, and fan engagement. By embracing AI responsibly and ethically, we can ensure that the benefits of AI in entertainment are realized for creators and audiences alike.

CHAPTER 31: AI IN CUSTOMER SERVICE

Overview

The integration of artificial intelligence (AI) in customer service is transforming the way businesses interact with their customers. AI-powered solutions enable companies to provide faster, more personalized, and efficient support, enhancing customer satisfaction and loyalty. This chapter explores the impact of AI on customer service, key applications, challenges, and future trends.

Impact of AI on Customer Service

1. **24/7 Availability:**

    ◦ AI-powered chatbots and virtual assistants provide round-the-clock customer support, ensuring that customers can get help whenever they need it. This availability reduces wait times and enhances customer satisfaction.

    ◦ **Benefits:** Increased customer satisfaction, reduced support costs, and improved response times.

2. **Personalized Customer Interactions:**

    ◦ AI analyzes customer data to provide personalized interactions and recommendations. By understanding customer preferences and behavior, AI can tailor responses and solutions to individual needs.

- ◦ **Benefits:** Enhanced customer experience, improved engagement, and higher conversion rates.

3. **Automated Query Resolution:**

- ◦ AI-powered systems can handle routine queries and tasks, such as checking account balances, updating personal information, and processing returns. This automation frees up human agents to focus on more complex issues.
- ◦ **Benefits:** Increased efficiency, reduced workload for human agents, and faster query resolution.

4. **Sentiment Analysis:**

- ◦ AI analyzes customer interactions to detect sentiment and emotions. This information helps businesses understand customer satisfaction, identify potential issues, and tailor responses accordingly.
- ◦ **Benefits:** Improved customer insights, proactive issue resolution, and enhanced customer loyalty.

5. **Proactive Support:**

- ◦ AI can predict potential issues and offer proactive support to customers. For example, AI can identify patterns that indicate a customer might be facing a problem and reach out with solutions before the customer contacts support.
- ◦ **Benefits:** Reduced customer frustration, increased customer loyalty, and enhanced brand reputation.

Key Applications of AI in Customer Service

1. **Chatbots:**
   - **Description:** AI-powered chatbots handle customer queries through text-based interactions. They can answer frequently asked questions, provide product information, and assist with common tasks.
   - **Examples:** Intercom, Drift, Chatfuel.

2. **Virtual Assistants:**
   - **Description:** AI-driven virtual assistants provide voice-based support to customers. They can perform tasks such as booking appointments, providing account information, and troubleshooting issues.
   - **Examples:** Amazon Alexa, Google Assistant, Apple Siri.

3. **Automated Email Responses:**
   - **Description:** AI systems analyze incoming emails and generate automated responses. These systems can categorize and prioritize emails, ensuring that urgent queries are addressed promptly.
   - **Examples:** Zoho Mail, Gmail's Smart Reply, Front.

4. **Sentiment Analysis Tools:**
   - **Description:** AI-powered sentiment analysis tools analyze customer interactions to detect emotions and sentiment. These tools help businesses understand customer satisfaction and tailor their responses.
   - **Examples:** MonkeyLearn, Lexalytics, IBM Watson Natural Language Understanding.

5. **Predictive Analytics:**

- **Description:** AI uses predictive analytics to anticipate customer needs and behaviors. This enables businesses to offer proactive support and personalized recommendations.
- **Examples:** Salesforce Einstein, Microsoft Dynamics 365 AI, Oracle AI.

6. **Voice Assistants:**

   - **Description:** AI-powered voice assistants handle customer queries through voice interactions. They can perform tasks such as checking order status, providing product information, and troubleshooting issues.
   - **Examples:** Nuance Nina, Google Contact Center AI, Amazon Lex.

Challenges of AI in Customer Service

1. **Data Privacy and Security:**

   - **Challenge:** Ensuring that customer data is protected and used responsibly, complying with data protection regulations such as GDPR and CCPA.
   - **Strategies:** Implement robust data protection measures, encrypt data, and ensure transparency in data usage.

2. **Bias and Fairness:**

   - **Challenge:** Addressing biases in AI algorithms that may lead to unfair treatment of certain customers or groups.
   - **Strategies:** Use diverse and representative datasets, conduct bias audits, and implement fairness-enhancing techniques.

3. **Natural Language Understanding:**

   - **Challenge:** Ensuring that AI systems accurately understand and interpret customer queries, particularly for complex or ambiguous requests.

- **Strategies:** Continuously improve natural language processing (NLP) models, use context-aware algorithms, and incorporate human-in-the-loop systems for complex queries.

4. **Customer Trust and Acceptance:**

- **Challenge:** Gaining customer trust and acceptance of AI-powered customer service solutions, particularly when transitioning from human to AI interactions.
- **Strategies:** Educate customers about AI, emphasize the benefits of AI-powered support, and ensure seamless handoffs to human agents when needed.

5. **Integration with Existing Systems:**

- **Challenge:** Integrating AI solutions with existing customer service systems and workflows can be complex and require significant investment.
- **Strategies:** Develop integration plans, use middleware solutions, and prioritize systems modernization.

Future Trends in AI in Customer Service

1. **Advanced NLP and Conversational AI:**

- AI will continue to advance in natural language processing and conversational capabilities, enabling more natural and human-like interactions with customers. This includes understanding context, detecting intent, and generating coherent responses.

2. **Emotionally Intelligent AI:**

○ AI systems will become more emotionally intelligent, capable of recognizing and responding to customer emotions and sentiments. This will enhance the quality of customer interactions and improve satisfaction.

3. **Multichannel AI Integration:**

○ AI will be integrated across multiple communication channels, including chat, email, voice, and social media. This will provide a seamless and consistent customer experience regardless of the channel used.

4. **AI-Driven Personalization:**

○ AI will enhance personalization by analyzing customer data and preferences to offer tailored recommendations, support, and marketing messages. This will drive higher engagement and conversion rates.

5. **Proactive and Predictive Support:**

○ AI will enable more proactive and predictive customer support by identifying potential issues before they arise and offering solutions preemptively. This will reduce customer frustration and enhance loyalty.

6. **Collaboration Between AI and Human Agents:**

○ The future of customer service will involve collaboration between AI and human agents. AI will handle routine tasks and queries, while human agents focus on complex and emotionally charged interactions. This collaboration will improve efficiency and customer satisfaction.

Conclusion

AI is transforming customer service by providing 24/7 availability, personalized interactions, automated query resolution, sentiment analysis, and proactive support. The integration of AI in customer service holds immense potential for improving efficiency, reducing costs, and enhancing customer satisfaction. However, it also presents challenges related to data privacy, bias, natural language understanding, customer trust, and system integration. By addressing these challenges and leveraging AI technologies, businesses can unlock new opportunities and drive innovation in customer service.

As we look to the future, the continued advancement of AI in customer service will further transform the industry, creating new possibilities for advanced NLP, emotionally intelligent AI, multichannel integration, AI-driven personalization, proactive support, and collaboration between AI and human agents. By embracing AI responsibly and ethically, businesses can ensure that the benefits of AI in customer service are realized for both customers and organizations.

CHAPTER 32: AI IN TRANSPORTATION AND LOGISTICS

Overview

The integration of artificial intelligence (AI) in transportation and logistics is revolutionizing how goods and people move from one place to another. AI technologies are enhancing efficiency, reducing costs, improving safety, and enabling new business models. This chapter explores the impact of AI on transportation and logistics, key applications, challenges, and future trends.

Impact of AI on Transportation and Logistics

1. **Enhanced Efficiency:**
   - AI optimizes route planning, fleet management, and supply chain operations, leading to more efficient use of resources and reduced operational costs.
   - **Benefits:** Reduced fuel consumption, minimized delays, and improved asset utilization.

2. **Improved Safety:**
   - AI-powered systems enhance safety in transportation by monitoring driver behavior, detecting hazards, and assisting in autonomous driving.

- **Benefits:** Reduced accidents, enhanced driver awareness, and increased overall safety on the roads.

3. **Predictive Maintenance:**

- AI enables predictive maintenance by analyzing data from vehicles and equipment to predict potential failures and schedule maintenance proactively.
- **Benefits:** Reduced downtime, extended lifespan of assets, and lower maintenance costs.

4. **Supply Chain Optimization:**

- AI optimizes supply chain operations by predicting demand, managing inventory, and coordinating logistics activities.
- **Benefits:** Reduced stockouts and overstock situations, improved customer satisfaction, and enhanced supply chain resilience.

5. **Autonomous Vehicles:**

- AI is driving the development of autonomous vehicles, including self-driving cars, trucks, and drones, which are set to transform transportation and delivery services.
- **Benefits:** Reduced labor costs, increased efficiency, and the potential for 24/7 operations.

Key Applications of AI in Transportation and Logistics

1. **Route Optimization:**

- **Description:** AI algorithms analyze real-time traffic data, weather conditions, and other factors to determine the most efficient routes for vehicles.
- **Examples:** Google Maps, Waze, UPS On-

Road Integrated Optimization and Navigation (ORION).

2. **Fleet Management:**
   - **Description:** AI-powered fleet management systems monitor vehicle health, driver behavior, and fuel consumption to optimize fleet operations.
   - **Examples:** Geotab, Fleet Complete, Samsara.

3. **Autonomous Driving:**
   - **Description:** AI enables the development of autonomous vehicles that can navigate and operate without human intervention, using sensors, cameras, and advanced algorithms.
   - **Examples:** Waymo, Tesla Autopilot, Nuro.

4. **Predictive Maintenance:**
   - **Description:** AI systems analyze data from sensors and IoT devices to predict equipment failures and schedule maintenance activities.
   - **Examples:** Uptake, Predikto, IBM Maximo.

5. **Warehouse Automation:**
   - **Description:** AI-driven robots and automation systems streamline warehouse operations, including picking, packing, and sorting.
   - **Examples:** Amazon Robotics, GreyOrange, Fetch Robotics.

6. **Last-Mile Delivery:**
   - **Description:** AI optimizes last-mile delivery by coordinating delivery routes, managing fleets of delivery vehicles, and ensuring timely deliveries.
   - **Examples:** Starship Technologies, Zipline, Postmates.

Challenges of AI in Transportation and Logistics

1. **Regulatory and Legal Issues:**
   - **Challenge:** Navigating the complex regulatory landscape for autonomous vehicles and AI-driven logistics solutions.
   - **Strategies:** Collaborate with regulatory bodies, stay informed about evolving regulations, and ensure compliance with local and international laws.

2. **Data Privacy and Security:**
   - **Challenge:** Ensuring the privacy and security of data collected from vehicles, sensors, and logistics operations.
   - **Strategies:** Implement robust data protection measures, encrypt data, and comply with data protection regulations.

3. **Integration with Legacy Systems:**
   - **Challenge:** Integrating AI solutions with existing transportation and logistics infrastructure can be complex and costly.
   - **Strategies:** Develop integration plans, use middleware solutions, and prioritize systems modernization.

4. **Public Acceptance:**
   - **Challenge:** Gaining public trust and acceptance of autonomous vehicles and AI-driven logistics solutions.
   - **Strategies:** Educate the public about the benefits of AI, conduct pilot programs, and ensure transparent communication.

5. **Skill Gaps:**
   - **Challenge:** Addressing the skill gaps in the workforce required to develop, deploy,

and maintain AI-driven transportation and logistics solutions.

- **Strategies:** Invest in training and education programs, collaborate with academic institutions, and promote continuous learning.

Future Trends in AI in Transportation and Logistics

1. **Expansion of Autonomous Vehicles:**
   - The deployment of autonomous vehicles will continue to expand, with advancements in AI enabling safer and more reliable self-driving cars, trucks, and drones.

2. **AI-Powered Urban Mobility:**
   - AI will enhance urban mobility by optimizing public transportation, reducing congestion, and promoting sustainable transportation solutions such as electric and shared vehicles.

3. **Integration of AI and Blockchain:**
   - The integration of AI and blockchain technology will enhance transparency, security, and efficiency in supply chain and logistics operations. Blockchain will provide a secure and immutable record of transactions, while AI will analyze data to optimize operations.

4. **Hyperloop and Advanced Transportation Systems:**
   - AI will play a crucial role in developing and operating advanced transportation systems such as the Hyperloop, which aims to revolutionize high-speed travel.

5. **Sustainable Logistics:**
   - AI will drive sustainability in logistics by optimizing routes, reducing emissions, and

promoting the use of renewable energy sources. AI-powered solutions will enable companies to achieve their sustainability goals.

6. **Smart Cities:**

   ◦ AI will contribute to the development of smart cities, where transportation and logistics systems are integrated and optimized using real-time data. This will lead to more efficient, sustainable, and connected urban environments.

Conclusion

AI is transforming transportation and logistics by enhancing efficiency, improving safety, enabling predictive maintenance, and driving the development of autonomous vehicles. The integration of AI in transportation and logistics holds immense potential for reducing costs, optimizing operations, and enhancing customer satisfaction. However, it also presents challenges related to regulatory compliance, data privacy, integration with legacy systems, public acceptance, and skill gaps. By addressing these challenges and leveraging AI technologies, the transportation and logistics industry can unlock new opportunities and drive innovation.

As we look to the future, the continued advancement of AI in transportation and logistics will further transform the industry, creating new possibilities for autonomous vehicles, urban mobility, blockchain integration, advanced transportation systems, sustainable logistics, and smart cities. By embracing AI responsibly and ethically, we can ensure that the benefits of AI in transportation and logistics are realized for businesses and society as a whole.

CHAPTER 33: AI IN AGRICULTURE

Overview

The integration of artificial intelligence (AI) in agriculture is transforming the way we grow, manage, and harvest crops. AI technologies are enhancing productivity, reducing resource consumption, and enabling precision farming. This chapter explores the impact of AI on agriculture, key applications, challenges, and future trends.

Impact of AI on Agriculture

1. **Precision Farming:**
   - AI enables precision farming by providing real-time data and analytics on crop health, soil conditions, and weather patterns. This allows farmers to make informed decisions and optimize resource use.
   - **Benefits:** Increased crop yields, reduced resource consumption, and improved sustainability.

2. **Automated Farming Operations:**
   - AI-powered robots and machinery automate various farming tasks, such as planting, irrigation, and harvesting. This reduces labor costs and increases efficiency.
   - **Benefits:** Enhanced productivity, consistent performance, and reduced labor dependency.

3. **Crop Monitoring and Management:**
   - AI systems use drones, sensors, and satellite imagery to monitor crop health, detect pests and diseases, and assess soil conditions. This enables timely interventions and better crop management.
   - **Benefits:** Early detection of issues, improved crop health, and optimized use of inputs.

4. **Supply Chain Optimization:**
   - AI optimizes the agricultural supply chain by predicting demand, managing inventory, and coordinating logistics. This ensures timely delivery of fresh produce and reduces food waste.
   - **Benefits:** Improved supply chain efficiency, reduced food waste, and better market access.

5. **Climate Resilience:**
   - AI helps farmers adapt to changing climate conditions by providing accurate weather forecasts, climate modeling, and risk assessments. This supports climate-resilient farming practices.
   - **Benefits:** Enhanced resilience to climate change, better risk management, and sustainable farming practices.

Key Applications of AI in Agriculture

1. **Precision Agriculture:**
   - **Description:** AI-driven precision agriculture uses data from sensors, drones, and satellite imagery to optimize farming practices, such as irrigation, fertilization, and pest control.
   - **Examples:** John Deere's Precision Agriculture, Climate FieldView, IBM Watson Decision

Platform for Agriculture.

2. **Autonomous Farm Machinery:**
   - **Description:** AI-powered autonomous machinery, such as tractors, drones, and harvesters, automate various farming tasks, reducing labor costs and increasing efficiency.
   - **Examples:** John Deere's autonomous tractors, AgEagle's agricultural drones, Fendt's IDEAL combine harvester.

3. **Crop Health Monitoring:**
   - **Description:** AI systems use computer vision and machine learning to analyze images from drones and satellites, detecting crop diseases, pests, and nutrient deficiencies.
   - **Examples:** DroneDeploy, Taranis, Xarvio Digital Farming Solutions.

4. **Soil and Weather Analysis:**
   - **Description:** AI analyzes soil samples and weather data to provide insights into soil health, moisture levels, and weather patterns. This information guides planting, irrigation, and fertilization decisions.
   - **Examples:** Arable, SoilCares, FarmLogs.

5. **Supply Chain Management:**
   - **Description:** AI optimizes the agricultural supply chain by predicting demand, managing inventory, and coordinating logistics. This ensures timely delivery of fresh produce and reduces food waste.
   - **Examples:** Descartes, ClearMetal, SmartFarm.

6. **Climate Modeling and Risk Assessment:**
   - **Description:** AI uses climate data and modeling to predict weather patterns, assess

climate risks, and support climate-resilient farming practices.

- ○ **Examples:** ClimateAI, The Climate Corporation, aWhere.

Challenges of AI in Agriculture

1. **Data Quality and Availability:**
   - ○ **Challenge:** Ensuring access to high-quality, accurate, and timely data for AI applications in agriculture.
   - ○ **Strategies:** Invest in data collection infrastructure, use advanced sensors and drones, and promote data sharing and collaboration.

2. **Cost and Affordability:**
   - ○ **Challenge:** High costs of AI technologies and their implementation can be a barrier for small and medium-sized farms.
   - ○ **Strategies:** Provide subsidies and financial support, develop cost-effective AI solutions, and promote cooperative models.

3. **Technical Expertise:**
   - ○ **Challenge:** Lack of technical expertise and knowledge among farmers to implement and maintain AI technologies.
   - ○ **Strategies:** Offer training and education programs, collaborate with agricultural extension services, and provide user-friendly AI tools.

4. **Data Privacy and Security:**
   - ○ **Challenge:** Protecting sensitive agricultural data and ensuring compliance with data protection regulations.
   - ○ **Strategies:** Implement robust data protection

measures, encrypt data, and ensure transparency in data usage.

5. **Integration with Traditional Practices:**
    - **Challenge:** Integrating AI technologies with traditional farming practices and ensuring acceptance among farmers.
    - **Strategies:** Promote the benefits of AI, involve farmers in the development process, and provide support for the transition.

Future Trends in AI in Agriculture

1. **Advanced Robotics and Automation:**
    - The future of AI in agriculture will see increased use of advanced robotics and automation, enabling tasks such as planting, weeding, and harvesting to be performed more efficiently and accurately.

2. **AI-Powered Decision Support Systems:**
    - AI-driven decision support systems will provide real-time insights and recommendations to farmers, helping them make informed decisions on crop management, resource use, and market access.

3. **Integration of AI and IoT:**
    - The integration of AI and the Internet of Things (IoT) will enable real-time monitoring and management of farming operations, enhancing efficiency and productivity.

4. **AI-Driven Crop Breeding:**
    - AI will play a crucial role in crop breeding by analyzing genetic data and predicting desirable traits, leading to the development of high-yield and resilient crop varieties.

5. **Sustainable Farming Practices:**

   ◦ AI will promote sustainable farming practices by optimizing resource use, reducing environmental impact, and supporting climate-resilient agriculture.

6. **Blockchain Integration:**

   ◦ The integration of AI and blockchain technology will enhance transparency, traceability, and trust in the agricultural supply chain, ensuring food safety and quality.

Conclusion

AI is transforming agriculture by enabling precision farming, automating farming operations, improving crop monitoring and management, optimizing the supply chain, and enhancing climate resilience. The integration of AI in agriculture holds immense potential for increasing productivity, reducing resource consumption, and promoting sustainable farming practices. However, it also presents challenges related to data quality, cost, technical expertise, data privacy, and integration with traditional practices. By addressing these challenges and leveraging AI technologies, the agriculture industry can unlock new opportunities and drive innovation.

As we look to the future, the continued advancement of AI in agriculture will further transform the industry, creating new possibilities for advanced robotics, decision support systems, AI and IoT integration, AI-driven crop breeding, sustainable farming practices, and blockchain integration. By embracing AI responsibly and ethically, we can ensure that the benefits of AI in agriculture are realized for farmers, consumers, and the environment.

CHAPTER 34: AI IN HEALTHCARE

Overview

Artificial intelligence (AI) is transforming healthcare by providing innovative solutions for diagnosing diseases, personalizing treatments, and improving patient outcomes. AI technologies are enhancing the efficiency, accuracy, and accessibility of healthcare services. This chapter explores the impact of AI on healthcare, key applications, challenges, and future trends.

Impact of AI on Healthcare

1. **Improved Diagnostics:**

   ◦ AI algorithms analyze medical images, patient data, and genetic information to detect diseases early and accurately. AI-powered diagnostic tools assist healthcare professionals in making informed decisions.

   ◦ **Benefits:** Increased diagnostic accuracy, early disease detection, and better patient outcomes.

2. **Personalized Medicine:**

   ◦ AI analyzes patient data to identify patterns and predict how individuals will respond to different treatments. This enables personalized treatment plans tailored to each patient's unique characteristics.

- **Benefits:** More effective treatments, reduced adverse effects, and improved patient satisfaction.

3. **Predictive Analytics:**

   - AI uses predictive analytics to identify patients at risk of developing certain conditions and to forecast disease progression. This allows for proactive interventions and better management of chronic diseases.
   - **Benefits:** Early intervention, improved disease management, and reduced healthcare costs.

4. **Enhanced Medical Imaging:**

   - AI enhances medical imaging by improving image quality, reducing noise, and assisting in the interpretation of scans. AI algorithms can detect anomalies and highlight areas of concern for radiologists.
   - **Benefits:** Improved image accuracy, faster diagnosis, and reduced workload for radiologists.

5. **Streamlined Administrative Tasks:**

   - AI automates administrative tasks such as scheduling appointments, managing patient records, and processing insurance claims. This reduces the administrative burden on healthcare providers and improves operational efficiency.
   - **Benefits:** Increased efficiency, reduced administrative costs, and more time for patient care.

Key Applications of AI in Healthcare

1. **AI-Powered Diagnostics:**
   - **Description:** AI algorithms analyze medical images, such as X-rays, MRIs, and CT scans, to detect diseases and abnormalities. These tools assist radiologists in making accurate diagnoses.
   - **Examples:** Zebra Medical Vision, Aidoc, PathAI.

2. **Predictive Analytics for Disease Prevention:**
   - **Description:** AI uses predictive analytics to identify patients at risk of developing chronic conditions, such as diabetes or heart disease, and recommend preventive measures.
   - **Examples:** IBM Watson Health, Health Catalyst, GNS Healthcare.

3. **Personalized Treatment Plans:**
   - **Description:** AI analyzes patient data, including genetic information and medical history, to develop personalized treatment plans tailored to individual needs.
   - **Examples:** Tempus, Foundation Medicine, Precision Health AI.

4. **Virtual Health Assistants:**
   - **Description:** AI-powered virtual health assistants provide patients with health advice, medication reminders, and answers to common medical questions.
   - **Examples:** Babylon Health, Ada Health, Your.MD.

5. **Robotic Surgery:**
   - **Description:** AI-powered robotic surgery systems assist surgeons in performing precise and minimally invasive procedures, reducing

recovery times and improving patient outcomes.

- **Examples:** Intuitive Surgical's da Vinci system, Medtronic's Hugo RAS system, Stryker's Mako system.

6. **Drug Discovery and Development:**

- **Description:** AI accelerates drug discovery by analyzing large datasets to identify potential drug candidates and predict their efficacy. This speeds up the development of new medications.
- **Examples:** BenevolentAI, Atomwise, Insilico Medicine.

Challenges of AI in Healthcare

1. **Data Privacy and Security:**

- **Challenge:** Ensuring the privacy and security of patient data, complying with regulations such as HIPAA (Health Insurance Portability and Accountability Act) and GDPR.
- **Strategies:** Implement robust data protection measures, encrypt data, and ensure transparency in data usage.

2. **Bias and Fairness:**

- **Challenge:** Addressing biases in AI algorithms that may lead to disparities in healthcare outcomes.
- **Strategies:** Use diverse and representative datasets, conduct bias audits, and implement fairness-enhancing techniques.

3. **Regulatory Compliance:**

- **Challenge:** Navigating the complex regulatory landscape for AI-driven healthcare solutions.

- **Strategies:** Stay informed about regulatory changes, collaborate with regulatory bodies, and ensure compliance with local and international laws.

4. **Integration with Existing Systems:**

- **Challenge:** Integrating AI solutions with existing healthcare systems, such as electronic health records (EHRs), can be complex and costly.
- **Strategies:** Develop integration plans, use middleware solutions, and prioritize systems modernization.

5. **Patient and Provider Acceptance:**

- **Challenge:** Gaining acceptance and trust from patients and healthcare providers for AI-driven healthcare solutions.
- **Strategies:** Educate stakeholders about the benefits of AI, involve them in the development process, and ensure transparent communication.

Future Trends in AI in Healthcare

1. **AI-Driven Telemedicine:**

- The future of AI in healthcare will see increased adoption of AI-driven telemedicine, enabling remote consultations, diagnostics, and monitoring. This will enhance access to healthcare services, especially in underserved areas.

2. **AI and Genomics:**

- AI will play a crucial role in genomics by analyzing genetic data to identify disease markers, predict disease risk, and develop personalized treatment plans based on genetic profiles.

3. **AI-Enhanced Wearable Devices:**
   - AI-powered wearable devices will continuously monitor vital signs, detect abnormalities, and provide real-time health insights. These devices will support proactive health management and early intervention.

4. **AI for Mental Health:**
   - AI will contribute to mental health by providing tools for early detection, monitoring, and intervention. AI-driven virtual therapists and mental health apps will offer support and resources to individuals.

5. **AI in Population Health Management:**
   - AI will enhance population health management by analyzing large datasets to identify trends, predict outbreaks, and develop targeted interventions to improve public health outcomes.

6. **AI and Robotics in Rehabilitation:**
   - AI-powered robotic systems will assist in rehabilitation, providing personalized therapy and tracking progress. These systems will enhance the effectiveness of rehabilitation programs.

Conclusion

AI is transforming healthcare by improving diagnostics, personalizing treatments, enhancing medical imaging, streamlining administrative tasks, and enabling predictive analytics. The integration of AI in healthcare holds immense potential for increasing efficiency, improving patient outcomes, and reducing costs. However, it also presents challenges related to data privacy, bias, regulatory compliance, integration, and acceptance. By addressing these challenges and leveraging

AI technologies, the healthcare industry can unlock new opportunities and drive innovation.

As we look to the future, the continued advancement of AI in healthcare will further transform the industry, creating new possibilities for AI-driven telemedicine, genomics, wearable devices, mental health, population health management, and robotics in rehabilitation. By embracing AI responsibly and ethically, we can ensure that the benefits of AI in healthcare are realized for patients, providers, and society as a whole.

CHAPTER 35: AI IN ENVIRONMENTAL SUSTAINABILITY

Overview

The growing urgency to address environmental challenges, such as climate change, deforestation, and pollution, has led to the integration of artificial intelligence (AI) in efforts to promote environmental sustainability. AI technologies are enhancing our ability to monitor, manage, and mitigate environmental impacts, enabling more sustainable practices across various sectors. This chapter explores the impact of AI on environmental sustainability, key applications, challenges, and future trends.

Impact of AI on Environmental Sustainability

1. **Climate Change Mitigation:**
   - AI is being used to model and predict climate patterns, enabling better understanding and mitigation of climate change impacts. AI-driven tools help optimize energy consumption, reduce greenhouse gas emissions, and promote renewable energy sources.
   - **Benefits:** Improved climate resilience, reduced carbon footprint, and enhanced sustainability.

2. **Biodiversity Conservation:**

   - AI supports biodiversity conservation by monitoring wildlife populations, detecting illegal activities like poaching, and analyzing ecosystems. AI-powered drones and sensors collect data in remote areas, providing valuable insights for conservation efforts.
   - **Benefits:** Protection of endangered species, preservation of ecosystems, and informed conservation strategies.

3. **Sustainable Agriculture:**

   - AI enhances sustainable agriculture by optimizing resource use, improving crop yields, and reducing environmental impact. AI-driven precision farming practices enable efficient water and fertilizer use, minimizing waste and pollution.
   - **Benefits:** Increased agricultural productivity, reduced resource consumption, and environmentally friendly farming practices.

4. **Pollution Monitoring and Management:**

   - AI technologies monitor air and water quality, detect pollution sources, and predict pollution levels. AI-driven systems analyze data from sensors and satellites to provide real-time insights and support pollution control measures.
   - **Benefits:** Improved environmental monitoring, early detection of pollution, and effective pollution management.

5. **Resource Efficiency:**

   - AI optimizes resource use in industries such as manufacturing, transportation, and construction. AI-driven systems analyze data to identify inefficiencies and recommend actions to reduce energy and material consumption.

- **Benefits:** Enhanced resource efficiency, reduced waste, and lower operational costs.

Key Applications of AI in Environmental Sustainability

1. **Climate Modeling and Prediction:**
   - **Description:** AI algorithms analyze climate data to model and predict climate patterns, assess the impact of climate change, and support mitigation strategies.
   - **Examples:** IBM's Green Horizon, Microsoft's AI for Earth, ClimateAI.

2. **Wildlife Monitoring and Conservation:**
   - **Description:** AI-powered drones, sensors, and camera traps monitor wildlife populations, detect poaching activities, and analyze habitats to support conservation efforts.
   - **Examples:** WildTrack, EarthRanger, Conservation Metrics.

3. **Precision Agriculture:**
   - **Description:** AI-driven precision farming practices optimize resource use, improve crop yields, and reduce environmental impact by using data from sensors, drones, and satellites.
   - **Examples:** John Deere's Precision Agriculture, Climate FieldView, FarmBot.

4. **Air and Water Quality Monitoring:**
   - **Description:** AI systems monitor air and water quality, detect pollution sources, and predict pollution levels using data from

sensors and satellites.

- **Examples:** AirVisual, BreezoMeter, H2O.ai.

5. **Energy Optimization:**

- **Description:** AI optimizes energy consumption in buildings, industries, and transportation by analyzing data and recommending actions to reduce energy use and promote renewable energy sources.
- **Examples:** Google's DeepMind, Verdigris, AutoGrid.

6. **Waste Management:**

- **Description:** AI-driven systems analyze waste data to optimize waste collection, recycling, and disposal processes, reducing environmental impact.
- **Examples:** AMP Robotics, Rubicon Global, ZenRobotics.

Challenges of AI in Environmental Sustainability

1. **Data Quality and Availability:**

- **Challenge:** Ensuring access to high-quality, accurate, and timely data for AI applications in environmental sustainability.
- **Strategies:** Invest in data collection infrastructure, use advanced sensors and drones, and promote data sharing and collaboration.

2. **Cost and Affordability:**

- **Challenge:** High costs of AI technologies and their implementation can be a barrier for widespread adoption.
- **Strategies:** Provide subsidies and financial support, develop cost-effective AI solutions, and promote public-private partnerships.

3. **Technical Expertise:**
   - **Challenge:** Lack of technical expertise and knowledge to implement and maintain AI technologies in environmental sustainability.
   - **Strategies:** Offer training and education programs, collaborate with academic institutions, and provide user-friendly AI tools.

4. **Data Privacy and Security:**
   - **Challenge:** Protecting sensitive environmental data and ensuring compliance with data protection regulations.
   - **Strategies:** Implement robust data protection measures, encrypt data, and ensure transparency in data usage.

5. **Ethical Considerations:**
   - **Challenge:** Addressing ethical concerns related to the use of AI in environmental sustainability, such as potential biases and unintended consequences.
   - **Strategies:** Conduct ethical impact assessments, involve diverse stakeholders, and ensure transparency in AI decision-making.

Future Trends in AI in Environmental Sustainability

1. **AI-Driven Climate Action:**
   - The future of AI in environmental sustainability will see increased use of AI to support climate action initiatives, including climate modeling, emission reduction strategies, and climate resilience planning.

2. **Integration of AI and IoT:**
   - The integration of AI and the Internet of

Things (IoT) will enable real-time monitoring and management of environmental conditions, enhancing data-driven decision-making and sustainability practices.

3. **AI for Circular Economy:**
    ◦ AI will play a crucial role in promoting a circular economy by optimizing resource use, reducing waste, and supporting recycling and reuse initiatives.

4. **AI-Enhanced Renewable Energy:**
    ◦ AI will enhance the efficiency and reliability of renewable energy sources, such as solar and wind power, by optimizing energy production, storage, and distribution.

5. **AI in Urban Sustainability:**
    ◦ AI will contribute to urban sustainability by optimizing transportation, energy use, and waste management in cities, leading to more sustainable and livable urban environments.

6. **Collaborative AI Platforms:**
    ◦ The development of collaborative AI platforms will enable stakeholders from different sectors to share data, insights, and best practices, fostering collective action for environmental sustainability.

Conclusion

AI is transforming environmental sustainability by supporting climate change mitigation, biodiversity conservation, sustainable agriculture, pollution monitoring, and resource efficiency. The integration of AI in environmental sustainability holds immense potential for addressing environmental challenges and promoting sustainable practices. However, it also presents challenges related to data quality, cost, technical expertise, data privacy, and ethical considerations.

By addressing these challenges and leveraging AI technologies, we can unlock new opportunities and drive innovation in environmental sustainability.

As we look to the future, the continued advancement of AI in environmental sustainability will further transform the field, creating new possibilities for AI-driven climate action, AI and IoT integration, circular economy initiatives, renewable energy optimization, urban sustainability, and collaborative AI platforms. By embracing AI responsibly and ethically, we can ensure that the benefits of AI in environmental sustainability are realized for the planet and future generations.

CHAPTER 36: AI IN MANUFACTURING

Overview

Artificial intelligence (AI) is revolutionizing the manufacturing industry by enabling smarter, more efficient, and more flexible production processes. AI technologies are transforming how products are designed, produced, and maintained, leading to increased productivity, reduced costs, and enhanced quality. This chapter explores the impact of AI on manufacturing, key applications, challenges, and future trends.

Impact of AI on Manufacturing

1. **Predictive Maintenance:**
   - AI-driven predictive maintenance systems use data from sensors and IoT devices to predict equipment failures before they occur. This allows manufacturers to perform maintenance proactively, reducing downtime and extending the lifespan of machinery.
   - **Benefits:** Reduced unplanned downtime, lower maintenance costs, and increased equipment reliability.

2. **Quality Control and Inspection:**
   - AI-powered quality control systems use computer vision and machine learning to detect defects and anomalies in products during the manufacturing process. These systems can identify issues in real-time and

ensure that only high-quality products reach the market.

- **Benefits:** Improved product quality, reduced waste, and enhanced customer satisfaction.

3. **Production Optimization:**

- AI optimizes production processes by analyzing data from various sources, such as production lines, supply chains, and market demand. AI algorithms can identify inefficiencies and recommend adjustments to improve productivity and reduce costs.
- **Benefits:** Increased production efficiency, reduced operational costs, and better resource utilization.

4. **Supply Chain Management:**

- AI enhances supply chain management by predicting demand, optimizing inventory levels, and coordinating logistics. AI-driven supply chain solutions provide real-time visibility and enable manufacturers to respond quickly to changes in demand and supply.
- **Benefits:** Improved supply chain resilience, reduced inventory costs, and better demand forecasting.

5. **Collaborative Robotics:**

- AI-powered collaborative robots (cobots) work alongside human workers to perform repetitive and physically demanding tasks. Cobots can adapt to changing environments and learn new tasks, increasing flexibility and productivity on the shop floor.
- **Benefits:** Enhanced worker safety, increased productivity, and improved flexibility in

manufacturing processes.

Key Applications of AI in Manufacturing

1. **Predictive Maintenance:**
   - **Description:** AI systems analyze data from sensors and IoT devices to predict equipment failures and schedule maintenance proactively.
   - **Examples:** Uptake, Augury, SparkCognition.

2. **Automated Quality Control:**
   - **Description:** AI-powered quality control systems use computer vision and machine learning to inspect products for defects and ensure high-quality standards.
   - **Examples:** Landing AI, Instrumental, Cogniac.

3. **Production Process Optimization:**
   - **Description:** AI optimizes production processes by analyzing data from production lines and identifying inefficiencies. AI algorithms recommend adjustments to improve productivity and reduce costs.
   - **Examples:** Siemens MindSphere, GE Digital's Predix, PTC's ThingWorx.

4. **Supply Chain Optimization:**
   - **Description:** AI enhances supply chain management by predicting demand, optimizing inventory levels, and coordinating logistics. AI-driven supply chain solutions provide real-time visibility and enable manufacturers to respond quickly to changes in demand and supply.
   - **Examples:** Llamasoft, ClearMetal, Kinaxis.

5. **Collaborative Robots (Cobots):**

- **Description:** AI-powered collaborative robots work alongside human workers to perform repetitive and physically demanding tasks. Cobots can adapt to changing environments and learn new tasks.
- **Examples:** Universal Robots, Rethink Robotics, FANUC.

6. **Generative Design:**

- **Description:** AI-driven generative design tools create optimized design solutions based on specified constraints and requirements. These tools explore a wide range of design possibilities and recommend the most efficient and effective designs.
- **Examples:** Autodesk's Generative Design, Siemens NX, Frustum.

Challenges of AI in Manufacturing

1. **Data Quality and Availability:**

- **Challenge:** Ensuring access to high-quality, accurate, and timely data for AI applications in manufacturing.
- **Strategies:** Invest in data collection infrastructure, use advanced sensors and IoT devices, and promote data sharing and collaboration.

2. **Integration with Legacy Systems:**

- **Challenge:** Integrating AI solutions with existing manufacturing systems and processes can be complex and costly.
- **Strategies:** Develop integration plans, use middleware solutions, and prioritize systems modernization.

3. **Cost and ROI:**

- **Challenge:** High costs of AI technologies and their implementation can be a barrier for some manufacturers. Ensuring a positive return on investment (ROI) is essential.
- **Strategies:** Identify high-impact use cases, conduct cost-benefit analyses, and leverage funding opportunities.

4. **Workforce Skills and Training:**
   - **Challenge:** Addressing the skill gaps in the workforce required to develop, deploy, and maintain AI-driven manufacturing solutions.
   - **Strategies:** Invest in training and education programs, collaborate with academic institutions, and promote continuous learning.

5. **Cybersecurity:**
   - **Challenge:** Protecting manufacturing systems and data from cyber threats and ensuring compliance with cybersecurity regulations.
   - **Strategies:** Implement robust cybersecurity measures, conduct regular security audits, and ensure compliance with industry standards.

Future Trends in AI in Manufacturing

1. **AI-Driven Autonomous Manufacturing:**
   - The future of AI in manufacturing will see increased adoption of fully autonomous manufacturing systems. AI-driven autonomous systems will handle end-to-end production processes, from design to delivery, with minimal human intervention.

2. **AI-Powered Smart Factories:**

- AI will enable the development of smart factories that use real-time data and advanced analytics to optimize production processes, improve quality, and reduce waste. Smart factories will be highly connected and adaptable to changing demands.

3. **AI and 3D Printing:**

   - The integration of AI and 3D printing will revolutionize manufacturing by enabling the production of complex and customized products on-demand. AI will optimize the design and production processes for 3D-printed parts.

4. **Sustainable Manufacturing:**

   - AI will promote sustainable manufacturing practices by optimizing resource use, reducing emissions, and supporting circular economy initiatives. AI-driven solutions will enable manufacturers to achieve their sustainability goals.

5. **Human-AI Collaboration:**

   - The future of manufacturing will involve seamless collaboration between human workers and AI-powered systems. AI will augment human capabilities, enhancing productivity and safety on the shop floor.

6. **AI-Enhanced Supply Chain Resilience:**

   - AI will enhance supply chain resilience by providing real-time visibility, predictive analytics, and dynamic optimization. AI-driven supply chain solutions will help manufacturers navigate disruptions and maintain continuity.

Conclusion

AI is transforming manufacturing by enabling predictive maintenance, improving quality control, optimizing production processes, enhancing supply chain management, and introducing collaborative robotics. The integration of AI in manufacturing holds immense potential for increasing productivity, reducing costs, and enhancing quality. However, it also presents challenges related to data quality, integration with legacy systems, cost and ROI, workforce skills, and cybersecurity. By addressing these challenges and leveraging AI technologies, the manufacturing industry can unlock new opportunities and drive innovation.

As we look to the future, the continued advancement of AI in manufacturing will further transform the industry, creating new possibilities for autonomous manufacturing, smart factories, AI and 3D printing integration, sustainable manufacturing, human-AI collaboration, and enhanced supply chain resilience. By embracing AI responsibly and ethically, we can ensure that the benefits of AI in manufacturing are realized for businesses, workers, and society as a whole.

ACKNOWLEDGEMENT

Writing this book has been an enriching journey, and I owe a debt of gratitude to many individuals and organizations whose support, guidance, and contributions have made this endeavor possible.

First and foremost, I would like to extend my heartfelt thanks to the AI research and development teams at Microsoft. Your pioneering work and dedication to advancing the field of artificial intelligence have been an invaluable source of inspiration and knowledge.

I am deeply grateful to the countless researchers, scientists, and engineers whose groundbreaking research and innovative solutions have shaped the AI landscape. Your work continues to push the boundaries of what is possible and drive progress in this exciting field.

To my colleagues and collaborators, your insights, feedback, and encouragement have been instrumental in shaping the content and direction of this book. Your expertise and passion for AI have enriched this work and made it a comprehensive resource for readers.

I would also like to acknowledge the support of my family and friends, who have been my pillars of strength throughout this journey. Your unwavering belief in me and your constant encouragement have been a source of motivation and inspiration.

A special thank you to the reviewers and editors who meticulously reviewed the manuscript and provided valuable feedback. Your attention to detail and commitment to excellence have greatly enhanced the quality of this book.

To the readers, thank you for your curiosity and enthusiasm for artificial intelligence. It is my hope that this book will serve as a valuable guide and resource as you explore the fascinating world of AI.

Finally, I would like to express my appreciation to all the individuals and organizations working towards the responsible and ethical development of AI. Your efforts to ensure that AI benefits humanity and addresses global challenges are truly commendable.

Thank you all for your contributions, support, and dedication. This book is a testament to the collective efforts of the AI community and the endless possibilities that lie ahead.